Dear
Sean Holland:

MW00939100

Happy Readings.

Don't forget
to
Stay Mindful

Jr. Allen

The
Mindfulness
RESPONSE

Inner Happiness Ever Day

Deborah C. Moore, Ph.D., LMFT

BALBOA.
PRESS
A DIVISION OF HAY HOUSE

Balboa Press books may be ordered through booksellers or by contacting:

Balboa Press
A Division of Hay House
1663 Liberty Drive
Bloomington, IN 47403
www.balboapress.com
1 (877) 407-4847

Because of the dynamic nature of the Internet, any web addresses or
links contained in this book may have changed since publication and
may no longer be valid. The views expressed in this work are solely those
of the author and do not necessarily reflect the views of the publisher,
and the publisher hereby disclaims any responsibility for them.

The author of this book does not dispense medical advice or prescribe the use
of any technique as a form of treatment for physical, emotional, or medical
problems without the advice of a physician, either directly or indirectly. The
intent of the author is only to offer information of a general nature to help you
in your quest for emotional and spiritual well-being. In the event you use any
of the information in this book for yourself, which is your constitutional right,
the author and the publisher assume no responsibility for your actions.

Any people depicted in stock imagery provided by Thinkstock are models,
and such images are being used for illustrative purposes only.
Certain stock imagery © Thinkstock.

Printed in the United States of America.

ISBN: 978-1-4525-2292-0 (sc)
ISBN: 978-1-4525-2294-4 (hc)
ISBN: 978-1-4525-2293-7 (e)
Library of Congress Control Number: 2014917555

Balboa Press rev. date: 10/17/2014

Dedication

This book is dedicated to all those seeking inner happiness.

Contents

Acknowledgments

*I*WOULD LIKE TO TAKE THIS TIME TO THANK ALL OF THE people who made this book possible. After years of self-neglect and neglecting important people in my life, I want to thank you for being patient with me during this process. I can honestly say I have now found balance in life and have developed inner happiness.

As a clinical therapist who has worked with hundreds of individuals and couples, I would like to thank my clients for allowing me to delve into their lives, to hear the most interesting details about their lives, and for allowing me to assist them in achieving balance and well-being, which allowed me to achieve that same balance as well. We learn from those we try to help and apply what we know and understand to ourselves. My clients have influenced me as I have influenced them. As I sat back in my chair giving out "homework assignments," I was exercising those same assignments in my life. Therapy is an exercise in risk-taking for both client and therapist. I became a model of change for my clients through the exercises I gave to them.

At times, therapists must be creative in assisting clients—thank you for allowing me to be spontaneous and creative in my approach. Creativity allowed me to become more energized, productive, and fresher in my perspective—all of which made me better able to help you.

INTRODUCTION

"The present moment is filled with joy and happiness. If you are attentive, you will see it." —Thích Nhất Hạnh, *Peace Is Every Step: The Path of Mindfulness in Everyday Life*

*H*APPINESS IS ALL AROUND US. LOOK AT THE TREES, NOTICE the beautiful flowers, and hear the whispers of the blowing wind. The world is sending each of us a message: "All you have to do is be open to it!"

I often share this perspective with new clients who have come to me for help in regaining a sense of balance in their lives. A common response is: "How can I possibly be happy when I am feeling so stressed?" This book is meant to answer that question. It's about the *how* of moving from feeling stressed to feeling happy and learning to appreciate all of life's precious moments. This book is about how you can learn to embrace life's challenges instead of avoiding them.

Most of us would agree that "feeling stressed" is the polar opposite of feeling happy. Yet stress is a necessary part of life, an opportunity for human development, a key to learning, and the potential spark that ignites both growth and creativity. Properly understood, stress is an essential and potentially positive factor in countless areas of our lives. The old saying "necessity is the mother of invention" could just as easily and accurately be stated: "Stress is the mother of invention."

It surprises my clients to hear it, but the reality is that some truly amazing things can happen in our lives if we manage to respond constructively to stress. By the same token though, whenever we *lose* the ability to respond to stress constructively, we pay a price. Sometimes that price is too high.

For a number of years, I have been working with people from all walks of life, face-to-face and eye-to-eye on stress management and stress coping issues. Each person had a unique, profoundly personal experience with the daily reality of stress. That is part of the nature of stress. Each of us experiences it in our own way.

It is also in the nature of stress that it sometimes causes us to lose track of what it does to us. That is certainly the case with my clients. Usually, they come to me because they are experiencing negative outcomes in their lives, and many of those outcomes connect to stress in ways they do not yet understand and have not learned to address healthily. For instance, they may be experiencing difficulty communicating effectively with coworkers, friends, or relatives. Very often, we find that improving the ability to manage day-to-day stress also improves the person's moment-to-moment experience of the relationship and his or her communication skills.

If you are reading these words, it is possible that you too are looking for help, guidance, and support in understanding the complex role that stress plays in your life, and you are also seeking to learn how you can achieve a sense of balance and well-being. It is possible that you too are looking for a better, more constructive way to deal with the stress you encounter in your daily life. I wrote this book because I am confident that the core principle I will be sharing with you, which I call the *"mindfulness response,"* can help you. It has helped hundreds of my clients. More importantly, research on mindfulness training suggests that individuals who use this approach develop better health and well-being.

Believe it or not, you already have everything you need right now to bring the mindfulness response into play in your own life in a noticeable, positive way. It is easier than you think to restore balance in your own life, and although it does take a little practice, you will begin to see results quickly. That is because you can start right away with what you have here and now.

Start with What You Have

"In this moment, there is plenty of time. In this moment, you are precisely as you should be. In this moment, there is infinite possibility."—Victoria Moran, *Younger by the Day: 365 Ways to Rejuvenate Your Body and Revitalize Your Spirit*

You may be thinking that mindfulness is difficult to achieve. But the truth is you do not need to be a Buddhist monk, or an expert meditator to engage in this process. No special advance training is necessary to see positive results with the mindfulness response. In fact, I recommend clients start with a beginners' mind.

At the beginning of the counseling process, my clients also tend to minimize the importance of changing their approach to stress. They are unaware of the negative physiological impacts that can accompany their failure to effectively cope with stress.

Usually, my clients are a little surprised to learn how profound the adverse effects are among people who have not learned to handle the stress in their lives. Maybe you will be surprised too.

The Health Impact

As a society, we have now gone a long way toward understanding, accepting, and responding appropriately to the dangers related to such activities as smoking, excessive drinking, and driving while under the influence of alcohol and drugs. For instance, it is far less socially acceptable today than it was in the 1970s to sell cigarettes or alcohol to minors. You may have also noticed the surge in commercial advertisements encouraging people to stop smoking or drinking alcohol. Why? Public awareness of these risks has increased. Now we know more than we used to about those risks. As a result, we have a clearer sense of how people can be hurt by smoking, drinking, and impaired driving. The risks of these activities are now more widely discussed than they were four decades ago. That is because we have initiated responsible, ongoing national discussions about these risks. The risks of smoking and drinking may always be with us, but we can approach them intelligently, which brings me to why I wrote this book. It is time—in fact, it is long past time—for a similar ongoing discussion of the significant health risks that are connected to mismanaged stress or improperly treated stress. As the title of the book implies: "*The Mindfulness Response: Inner Happiness Every Day!*" mindfulness is the cornerstone for fulfilled human existence.

As human beings we are wired to seek happiness and pleasure and to avoid stress and unhappiness. When stress is not managed properly, it can cause psychological as well as physiological problems. In a Lanka newspaper article on December 04, 2010, R. Morgan Griffith identifies the following clinically documented health risks. All are connected to poor management of daily stressors.

Heart disease. Emotional stress can be a trigger for serious heart problems. People with chronic heart issues are at significant unnecessary risk for major health crises if they do not learn to manage the stress in their lives effectively.

Asthma. Multiple studies have demonstrated that stress can exacerbate asthmatic problems.

Diabetes. Poorly managed stress has been correlated with elevated glucose levels in people with type 2 diabetes.

Decreased immunity. How often have you had a cold or the flu after you have experienced a stressful period in your life? Research suggests prolonged stressful experiences can decrease the effectiveness of your immune system. The immune system is the body's defense that fights off bacteria, viruses, and other foreign or toxic substances.

Years ago, researchers believed that the immune system was a totally independent bodily system with no input from the brain and that it was certainly not influenced by one's thoughts. In the mid-1970s, psychologists and immunologists found evidence of a mind/body connection—that psychological factors such as one's thoughts, influence the immune system.

Dramatically reduced life expectancy. A 2012 study demonstrated a clear cause-and-effect relationship between chronic stress and dramatically lower life spans. The evidence from a variety of studies, including one cited in Griffith's (2010) newspaper article, seems to suggest that unaddressed problems with stress can shave as much as seventeen years off your life span.

How is this possible? Elizabeth Blackburn, a Yale graduate, and her colleagues discovered the function of telomeres. Chromosomes are protected by telomeres, which resemble cap-like structures. Over the course of our life span, telomeres will shorten. The shortening of telomeres is usually a result of the body's natural aging process. Aging, mortality, and age-related diseases can cause telomeres to shorten. An interesting discovery has led researches to examine the correlation between chronic stress and the shortening of these protectors. When we are experiencing a tremendous amount of stress, we are actually shortening our life span, as our telomeres decrease in size. In addition to reduced life span, there are many negative physiological impacts connected to poor stress management, including cardiovascular problems, hypertension, greater susceptibility to infection, skin problems, and diabetes.

It's clear that the discussion about stress is an important one. Perhaps you are wondering why I've written this book about addressing everyday *stress* with the conscious practice of *mindfulness* and the promotion of *happiness*. Although mindfulness has been getting more and more attention in recent years, the topic of how stress relates to mindfulness and happiness remains under-discussed in our society.

Current research suggests that when our minds wander we are usually thinking about unpleasant things. For this reason it is better to stay focused on the moment. Taking a few minutes each day to clear your mind through the art of mindfulness meditation is the simplest, most effective way of constructively addressing everyday stress and creating inner happiness.

For years, people have tried a wide variety of tactics to reduce stress, including physical exercise, changes in diet, listening to various types of music, and so on. As positive as these behavioral changes might be in their own right, my experiences with my clients suggest that they leave out an important part of the equation: the person's conscious assessment of his or her own situation.

Your personal assessment of the situation is the first step in stress reduction. When this comes first, the pattern of stress reduction is easier to implement, easier to return to, and more effective at reducing unhealthy responses to everyday stress over time. I am not saying that you should not exercise, make better choices about what you eat, or find good music to listen to. All I am suggesting is that I have personally found that this simple tactic of reframing the way the mind processes stressful events has been the most effective method. It has delivered lasting positive results to the vast majority of my own clients ... and to me as well!

The practice of mindfulness, which you will learn about here, does not take the place of one-on-one counseling, and it is not a cure-all for all the kinds of stress one can experience. But it is an important tool in the toolbox, a tool that we could and should be using to deal with the epidemic of poorly managed stress in our society. Not only does mindfulness training improve emotional and psychological stability, it has also been shown to improve other areas of health. For instance, in her June 14, 2012 Huffington Post article, Amanda Chan outlines two benefits that the practice of mindfulness can bring: Reduces the impact of cold and flu symptoms and improves sleep patterns. Other benefits of mindfulness practice include:

- Lower health care costs overall (National Center for Biotechnology Information, 2014).
- Increased brain development in areas associated with learning, memory, and self-control.
- Establishes a direct pathway to conscious decision making.
- Decrease pain and chronic inflammation.

In this book, I will ask you to think just a little differently. I'll show you how to handle common stressful situations much more effectively. It may take a little time and a little practice to learn how to change existing patterns, but it is definitely worth the effort.

Performing the activities I will share with you in this book, for as little as ten minutes a day, will leave you better equipped to handle the hassles of everyday life and to promote inner happiness. You will be able to deal with challenging situations more effectively. And you will be happier and healthier. Why? Because once you are able to handle the little, everyday stresses more effectively, you will be better positioned to handle major stress. There is no shortage of either kind of stress in our lives, so it is up to us to learn the most constructive responses.

Let me reiterate a critical point. We *must* learn to respond constructively to stress for the simple reason that failing to do so literally reduces our life span.

I close this introduction hoping that this book will begin the constructive, ongoing national and global discussion we need to have about the risks associated with stress and how to promote inner happiness. With that kind of discussion, we can, as a society, increase our understanding about the serious physiological effects of stress, raise our awareness about the different kinds of stress, and harness the powerful coping strategy of mindfulness. Moreover, you will live a happier and healthier life.

It is easier than you may think. You are stronger than you think. Remember ... *If you want to be happy, you can be happy!*

CHAPTER 1

Major! Minor! Mindful!

You must learn to let go. Release the stress. You were never in control anyway.—Steve Maraboli

WHAT IS STRESS? This is a useful, pragmatic definition of stress. Stress has a lot to do with what we feel. It is the anxious or threatening feeling that comes when we appraise a situation as being more than our physical, emotional, or psychological resources can adequately handle. Notice the key word: *appraise*. Stress is rooted in our *appraisal* of what is happening to us.

Most researchers define stress as any situation in which we perceive the demands of a situation as exceeding our ability to effectively cope with that situation.

A **stressor** is something that causes stress.

"As we encounter new experiences with a mindful and wise attention, we discover that one of three things will happen to our new experience: it will go away, it will stay the same, or it will get more intense."—Jack

Kornfield, *A Path with Heart: A Guide Through the Perils and Promises of Spiritual Life*

Appraisal is a deeply personal experience, because people experience stress in different ways; this is the fundamental reality of

> **Appraisal** is the process by which people make judgments about what is happening to them. Our appraisal of our situation has a huge impact on the way we process the demands of potentially stressful events. It also affects how we cope with those demands.

stress. It is personal and rooted in what is taking place in our lives. Our responses to stress are also personal. For example, you have just learned you are going to be relocating to a new city, someplace you have never lived before. For some people, the prospect of moving to a

brand-new place can be an instantly overwhelming experience, one that can produce significant amounts of what they might describe as stress. Packing, arranging for movers, expenses, exploring new doctors, making new friends, changing schools, or finding a new job are issues to consider when relocating. Just thinking about moving can leave someone feeling overwhelmed and exhausted, perhaps even mentally incapacitated.

On the other hand, someone else could view this same event as an entirely positive "new chapter" in life—a challenge to be met and overcome, something to welcome and learn from. For this person, a move to a new city could be seen as a significant avenue for personal growth. Because of an optimistic attitude, this person may have a reaction to the event that is very different from that of the person who is feeling anxious and overwhelmed. But here is the part we often overlook:

We have more control over how we experience such situations than we think.

If you consider a move to another city to be a debilitating, exhausting ordeal, you may recognize your own reactions to that situation. You can learn to change your thinking and feeling about that situation in order to cope effectively. With a little practice and time, you can change your reaction to potentially stressful events. You can learn how to *respond* rather than *react*.

The ability to respond constructively to stress is an important life skill, because stress is both ubiquitous and potentially dangerous to us. No matter who you are, eventually you will experience something that is personally stressful. Whether it is sitting in traffic, getting married, going through a divorce, looking for a new job, waiting in a doctor's office, struggling to make financial ends meet, caring for a sick family member, or waiting for an airplane to take off, you will experience a situation that makes you doubt your ability to handle it. This is part of the human developmental process.

Each of us can learn this lifesaving skill, but there is a catch: we must do so as individuals, knowing our own unique strengths and blind spots. We must approach challenges with a willingness to be fully present in our own lives. That process can begin for you right now!

Most of us get into the habit of poisoning ourselves with stress, anxiety, and fear. Why? Because we have not learned how to establish balance, inner happiness, and peace in our lives or within ourselves.

Happiness is a state of mind. It involves taking full responsibility for our own thoughts, words, and actions. Speaking of taking responsibility, consider this important quote:

> "Nothing can do us more harm than a thought unguarded."—The Buddha

Based on my experience as both a licensed clinical therapist and retired law-enforcement officer, I observed that the human mind is either a great ally or a dangerous adversary. With just a little practice, we can ensure that it is our ally. Take a minute to ask yourself: *Is my mind my best friend or my worst enemy?*

In order to establish balance in our own lives, we must to practice guarding our own thoughts. This practice is what allows us to develop *productive* responses to stressful events.

Most of us do not have much practice when it comes to guarding our thoughts from the events that unfold before us. Typically, we react to the incidents in our lives that cause stress (stressors). Usually, we react pretty heedlessly. *Reacting* rather than *responding* only enhances the lack of balance in our lives, making it all the more difficult to reestablish our natural state of balance. All too often, we allow our unguarded thoughts to control our feelings and behaviors.

It is very easy to react rather than respond to the stressors in our lives. At times, it seems we live in an unbalanced and generally unhappy world. The reality is that there are a lot of potential stressors out there. We do not have a lot of practice responding mindfully to stress. Yet, if we pay attention, we will notice that the stressors we encounter are not all equal. Noticing this is an excellent point of entry.

Creating the balance necessary to respond consciously to the stressors in our lives requires understanding and patience, something most people do not have. Human beings experience two very different kinds of stress. In order to respond consciously to either kind of stress, it helps to have a sense of which kind of stressor you are facing. Let us set the stage for your own mindful response to the stressors in your life by looking at the two main kinds of stress and how to distinguish between them clearly.

Two Kinds of Stress

Consider these two lists of potential stressors:

List A
A wedding
A divorce

The death of a close family member
The serious, long-term illness of a family member
The serious physical injury of a family member
The loss of a job
The loss of a home
A major financial setback, such as bankruptcy
An undesired/unprepared-for/unexpected move to a new city
The trauma of being involved in a serious accident

List B
Sitting in slow or unmoving traffic
Waiting for a repair person
Waiting for medical results
Congestion of daily commuting
Waiting in line
Dealing with difficult coworkers or supervisors
Dealing with short-term relationship issues, such as a conflict over an interaction with one's in-laws at a holiday gathering
Dealing with short-term financial challenges, such as the loss of a big sale you were counting on

Which kind of stressor do you think has the potential to do more to make you sick? List A? List B?

Whenever I ask that question, most people respond that they think List A has the greater potential to make them sick. Actually, though, the greatest potential health dangers are the seemingly minor stressors found in List B. Why?

The items on List A are **major stressors,** the major life events that typically do not occur often in life. We

Major stressors are potentially disturbing, troubling, or disruptive events, either positive or negative, that we appraise as having a significant impact on our lives. They don't happen every day.

5

can come to terms with major stressors and even learn and grow from them.

Major stressors often carry some of life's most important lessons. There are certainly trials, struggles, and painful moments that accompany our experience of them, and they may sometimes take significant time to work through. They happen, and then they pass. Once they do, we may find ourselves better, wiser, and more experienced people. Adjusting successfully to major stressors is one of the hallmarks of healthy adulthood. Unless there is some underlying problem, we probably will not experience long-term psychological scars as a direct result of a move to a new city. Rather, *we adapt* to the change, and *we move on.* The same is true of bigger (but functionally identical) major stressors, such as divorce or the loss of a loved one. While there are certainly situations where people find themselves overwhelmed by traumatic stress, major stressors are something we experience and move beyond.

By contrast, you may well spend a couple of hours each day, for three years (or thirty), muttering under your breath about how much you hate the morning traffic. You can work yourself into a stressful state day after day until it literally becomes part of your lifestyle. This is an example of a minor stressor.

Minor stressors are ordinary, common sources of stress, rather than an extraordinary set of events. They arise from something that irritates us. They do not have a life-changing impact and may or may not occur repeatedly.

Typically, we all face minor stressors during the course of a single day. I call these stressors "routine hassles of everyday living," because, unlike major stressors, they happen quite frequently during the course of an average day.

Someone cuts us off in traffic. We miss an important flight. Someone says something rude to us at work. A pattern of unhealthy communication emerges between you and your significant other. There are dozens, hundreds, of potential minor stressors that we each face on a regular basis. Whether we react heedlessly to these minor stressors or learn to respond consciously to them will have a major impact on the quality of our life and health.

Here is the point to remember. When minor stressors become acute (that is, of short, intense duration), these experiences of life's daily hassles actually do more to make people sick than major life changes. Minor stressors may seem like they have less of an impact. However, they do have a cumulative effect ... and they can interact with major stressors in complex ways. It is not uncommon for poorly managed minor stressors to cause a reduction in overall health and immune function. This leaves us at risk for more serious impacts from diseases we might otherwise be able to fight off without difficulty.

If we do not learn to manage them properly, major stressors and minor stressors can reinforce each other in ways that significantly compromise our ability to be resilient in many areas of life.

"Mindfulness is simply being aware of what is happening right now without wishing it were different; enjoying the pleasant without holding on when it changes (which it will); being with the unpleasant without fearing it will always be this way (which it won't)."—James Baraz

Minor Stressor Alert!

So this is the paradox. Potentially, minor stressors carry more serious health risks than major stressors. This is because ...

a) Minor stressors may happen over and over again, and unhealthy reactions to them may even come to be perceived as "normal." If you spend two out of twenty-four furious at the traffic you navigate on your way to and from work, that is not something you should consider "normal," even though you may have grown used to it.

b) They may leave us less able to handle major stressors when they eventually do materialize in our lives. This is a point we must not minimize. It is part of the human experience to encounter major stressors. It is not a question of *whether* these experiences will come our way but *when*. We need to be ready to respond resourcefully to them when they do appear.

Fortunately, you can avoid both of these outcomes just by getting better at handling the everyday hassles in your life—the minor stressors. This is easier than you may think.

So let me use this part of the book to set some objectives. This book is about learning to handle *minor stressors* in a healthy way. It is not about creating a vaccination for avoiding major life events. But ... if you follow the advice that I share with you here and do the exercises that I outline, you will automatically position yourself to handle the minor stressors you will experience in life in a healthier way.

There is no escaping stress in human life. There is only the navigation of stress. The way you navigate daily stress either impedes your growth as a person or supports that growth. Without stress you never would have learned to walk or feed yourself or interact with others or make any kind of contribution to anyone, including yourself. Stress is part of how we learn and grow. But it does not have to be and should not be how we die.

Mindfulness can literally make the difference between life and death when it comes to processing the stressors we encounter on a daily basis.

The real challenge is not the everyday hassle of life or the stressor that you experience; although it sometimes seems that way. It is how we appraise the experience. Our past histories can sometimes affect the way we perceive certain stressors. But overcoming this is only a matter of practice.

"This Sounds Difficult."

Most people who hear me discuss this subject imagine that the mindfulness techniques I describe are going to be very difficult to master ... but this is usually because they have never actually attempted to practice mindfulness. They confuse the stressful event they haven't yet navigated with the practice of mindfulness. The thing that is actually difficult to change is the external event that causes a stressful reaction, such as a traffic jam. The traffic jam is a stressor. No amount of mental effort (that I am aware of, at any rate) can magically transform a traffic jam into an empty expressway. However, it is not the stressor that we are interested in transforming. It is what we choose to do with our attention once we encounter the stressor that matters, and that is indeed within our control.

Once we internalize this distinction, mindfulness becomes more accessible.

The real challenge is whether we will react heedlessly or respond consciously to the stressor we encounter. An important part of this distinction involves learning to recognize minor stressors when they arise in our lives—and they will!

Before you move on to the next chapter ... answer these questions.

*On a separate sheet of paper, or in a notebook, jot down five "daily hassles" from the past week that have produced stress in your own life. These should be events that do repeat or could repeat on a daily or weekly basis, not one-time challenges.

*Next, jot down your most recent "life event" stressor. This should be a significant, life-altering event that caused you major personal stress and that would not happen in quite the same way ever again, such as the death of a loved one, the loss of a job, or the end of an important relationship.

CHAPTER 2

Keeping It Real: The Facts about Stress

"Respond; don't react.
Listen; don't talk.
Think; don't assume."
—Raji Lukkoor

*Y*OU DO NOT HAVE TO BE A PROFESSIONAL IN THE FIELD OF stress management to grasp that there are a lot of misconceptions, incomplete pieces of information, and plain old doubletalk about the reality of stress.

Sometimes it seems as though stress is both the most—and least—understood topic of modern time. One thing is clear enough: we all experience stress, and most of us could do a better job of managing with it.

In this chapter, we will look at a number of particularly widespread misconceptions about stress that can keep people from adopting a healthy, mindful approach to stress management in their daily lives.

Misconception #1: All stress is equal. People sometimes think that stress is something universally experienced in more or less the same way by everyone. In fact, what serves as a significant or even debilitating stressor for me might not be much of a stressor for someone else. As I previously stated, the experience of stress turns out to be deeply personal. In fact, it is unique to each individual, and whether we consider it "good" or "bad" in nature is deeply personal as well. Here is an example. For some people, the idea of picking up a telephone and talking to a total stranger about whether or not he or she will consider doing business with their company is absolutely terrifying. This kind of experience is known as a "cold call." Other people might describe the same discussion as "networking" and "business development," and it gives them motivation and a challenge that gets them going, day after day. This common example offers us the perfect transition into misconception number two.

Misconception #2: All stress is bad. As you learned a little earlier in this book, stress is actually an important part of the human experience, something that each of us has used, continue to use, and will keep on using if we are healthy enough to keep on growing and surviving. Without stress you would never have learned how to ride a bicycle, deal with potentially unpleasant people, make a deadline at work, finish college, or even become successful in your field. Ideally, we learn from the stressors we encounter during the day, and some of those stressors fall into a special category known as *eustress*.

So perhaps for me, the act of picking up the telephone, talking to a total stranger, and asking for an appointment is something I would try hard to avoid. For you, it is *eustress*. That does not make the situation right or wrong; it just allows us to have different responses

Eustress is a stressor that we perceive as being positive, for example getting married or getting a job promotion. This standard is likely to be distinct to each individual.

to the situation. There are plenty of things that are stressful for us; however, they produce a favorable, more desirable outcome. We see these events as a positive challenge. For example, the birth of a child may be initially stressful, but the outcome is met with joy.

Misconception #3: Stress is a mental and emotional issue that has no major physical implications. We have already looked at this in the Introduction, but it is worth reexamining. This is the misconception that I am most likely to encounter during early discussions with clients about managing stress. They simply do not make a correlation between the chronic, unmanaged, negative stress they are experiencing on a daily basis and the accompanying negative physical outcomes that they encounter in their lives. I have seen many people simply tune out discussions about the role of stress as it connects to serious problems with their physical health. Moreover, stress can affect their interpersonal relationships, their psychological resilience, and their overall ability to enjoy life.

I had a recent client who had a very demanding job that took him all over the world. That work schedule had been placing significant demands on his ability to cope for years. He also had to deal with a major personal crisis. His mother, who had recently turned eighty, had become frail and was now having some health problems. So in addition to an insane travel schedule, which he was having a hard time keeping up, he now had his mother's medical issues to deal with on a daily basis. This man's body was shutting down! Of course, he was encountering minor stressors and major stressors simultaneously, and he was not adjusting well to any of it! I had to spend a significant amount of time, effort, and energy in order to make him aware that the way he was mismanaging his daily stress was part of the reason he was having physical, emotional, career, and interpersonal problems in his life ... all at the same time. The pattern is a common one, so common that I have to reiterate here that unmanaged chronic stress does carry serious health implications. In his case, it compromised his immune system and brought on a case of shingles. That was not his only problem by any means. The only way we were able to turn the situation around for him was for me to help him recognize that poorly managed chronic stress was in fact a huge contributing factor. That conversation took a while, because this subject was anathema to him. But fortunately we got where we needed to go. He mastered the mindfulness response you will learn here, and he reclaimed some balance in his life.

The message here is quite simple. We all need a "reality check" moment. We must accept the reality that poorly handled stress really does take a toll on us physically, and we really do have to learn to manage it properly. This is not optional. For some of my clients that "reality check" moment is relatively easy. For others, it is a much more difficult process. One of the reasons I wrote this book was to make overcoming this misconception easier for my clients and everyone else.

Misconception #4: Stress is something you can and should avoid. Many people are under the assumption that stress is a disease that should be avoided. Let me emphasize once again that stress is part of the human development process. We are all human, and that means we all have to deal with stress at some point in our lives.

Your day consists of many business meetings. You have a busy day scheduled, with several appointments on the calendar involving a number of your most important clients. You come out of your first meeting of the day, which did not go well, and you know you have a very tight window to get to your *next* meeting. You sprint to your car, and you notice that one of your tires is flat as a pancake. Of course, that stresses you out! That is a natural reaction. It would stress virtually anyone out. Congratulations: you have just encountered a minor stressor.

At first you will probably react the same way your knee reacts when you hit it with a rubber hammer … a knee-jerk reaction. Just about all of us react rather than respond to those initial firestorms of neural reactions we experience when we encounter a minor stressor or something that is out of our control. In this flat-tire situation, for instance, we might instantly think something like "*Why me? This should not be happening to me.*" That is a natural reaction. The trick is not to avoid reacting. The trick is to notice when you *do* react, so you can get in the habit of responding consciously to your environment. In this case, for instance, you might notice that the question "*Why me?*" was not going to get you any closer to where you wanted to be, and then ask yourself a better set of questions: "*What am I looking at here, and what needs to happen next?*"

Misconception #5: Positive thinking is something new. In responding to minor stressors, I will ask you to use a technique you may recognize as a variation on "positive thinking." Most of us hear the term "positive thinking" and immediately associate it with "positive psychology" or "psychology of happiness." In actuality, the term "positive thinking" is pretty *old* thinking. According to Psychology Today magazine (2014), the term appeared as a reference to therapeutic spirituality in the title of a book published in 1864. The nineteenth-century author considered suffering an illusion and held that happiness can result from what he called "right-thinking." Various philosophical and religious systems have put forward similar ideas. The Buddhists and Taoists have been doing so for centuries.

Misconception #6: We can't think our way through stressful times. Most of my clients (initially) fall prey to this misconception. They imagine that the stressor itself is the problem and that no change in thinking can affect their situation. They get distracted by external events. Current research suggests that we can indeed think our way through the tough times we encounter. Researchers have now examined how our thoughts literally affect our reality and have found some remarkable correlations between what we think and how we handle stress.

In the field of neuropsychology, researchers have determined that the way we think can play a role in self-improvement and even produce physical changes in our brains. In fact, we can retrain our nerve cells or neurons to have a long-term relationship with one another. If we practice positive and healthy thinking, eventually these nerve cells will strengthen and become our habitual response to situations. Nerve cells that fire together wire together!

Those are some of the most common myths about stress. Some of them have been remarkably persistent through the years. I have tried to shed some light on the realities beneath the myth. My hope is that by sharing this chapter with you, I have helped you to move past the most common barrier to effective stress management: your own belief system.

> "If you are reading these words, perhaps it is because something has kicked open the door for you and you are ready to embrace change. It is not enough to appreciate change from afar, or only in the abstract, or as something that can happen to other people but not to you. We need to create change for ourselves, in a workable way, as part of our everyday lives."
> —Sharon Salzberg, *Real Happiness: The Power of Meditation: A 28- Day Program.*

CHAPTER 3

Do I Have to Chant?

"Feelings, whether of compassion or irritation, should be welcomed, recognized, and treated on an absolutely equal basis; because both are ourselves. The tangerine I am eating is me. The mustard greens I am planting are me. I plant with all my heart and mind. I clean this teapot with the kind of attention I would have were I giving the baby Buddha or Jesus a bath. Nothing should be treated more carefully than anything else. In mindfulness, compassion, irritation, mustard green plant, and teapot are all sacred." —Thích Nhất Hạnh, *The Miracle of Mindfulness: An Introduction to the Practice of Meditation*

So WHAT HAVE WE LEARNED SO FAR? We have learned that there are different types of stressors, minor and major. Minor stressors, which are primarily what this book is about, are the everyday hassles of life. Major stressors, on the other hand, are usually rare lifetime transitions (like job loss, death, or serious illness) that can present major obstacles for us.

We have learned that our ability to handle minor stressors in a healthy way can have a major positive impact on our ability to handle major stressors. Handling stress constructively improves our physical health and overall quality of life.

In addition, we have learned that we should not imagine that we are going to live a stress-free life. That is simply not possible. Stress is part of human existence and plays a role in our growth and development. The question is not how we can eliminate stress from our existence but rather how we can embrace it and develop more effective ways of dealing with it—all of which brings us to the point of this chapter and the book as a whole, which is mindfulness.

Most people are initially a little hesitant when I start talking about mindfulness training as a stress-management technique and a road to enter happiness. They tend to assume that they have to learn special mantras, chant, stand on their heads, or perform some strange rituals.

Actually, what I am talking about is much more pragmatic and accessible. Mindfulness is simply being present in the moment. Mindfulness is the art of noninterference, not clinging to anything or striving to be anywhere else. It means simply being there.

Although mindfulness can be traced to Buddhist and Taoist meditation principles, there is no need to be familiar with either of those traditions in order to benefit from it. There is no religious dimension to what I will be sharing with you in this book, unless you choose to add that dimension yourself (which, of course, you are free to do). We are not talking about a cultural, religious, or spiritual conversion here. We are talking about a coping skill and tool to promote inner happiness and peace. The mindfulness response can improve your health, inner well-being, and interpersonal relationships.

The technique of mindfulness meditation is both ancient and modern. Mindfulness is fairly easy to learn and implement on the beginner's level. However, it is always a lifelong process. All you need for what we will be doing in this book is a "beginner's mind," which is all that I have ever claimed to pursue for myself and my clients. The mindfulness approach has received more attention in recent years. People are seeking a higher power of intervention to help them cope with minor as well as major stressors. This power is one that comes from within or from a spiritual process.

Mindfulness 101

The very first step in any personal stress-management approach should incorporate mindfulness training. By that I mean simply that we should follow these three steps to create a "pattern interrupt" whenever we find ourselves in the middle of an instinctive reaction to one of life's daily hassles. It is easy to react to stressors, but by following these three steps, we can begin the process by which we can actually *respond* to the situation consciously.

Mindfulness is easier than you think. The three mindfulness steps are:

Step 1: Accept. Look at yourself and the situation you are in without judgment, and recognize that nothing in it is either good or bad. You are simply what you are. Whatever is happening is simply what it is. I cannot overemphasize how important it is for us to take step one and initiate acceptance consciously so we can begin the mindfulness process.

> "The most fundamental aggression to ourselves, the most fundamental harm we can do to ourselves, is to remain ignorant by not having the courage and the respect to look at ourselves honestly and gently."
> —Pema Chödrön, *When Things Fall Apart: Heart Advice for Difficult Times*

Step 2: Breathe and notice. As you breathe, become aware of what you are currently experiencing physically and mentally. Usually this involves using our five senses: sight, sound, touch, taste, and smell. If you feel discomfort in your stomach or feel dryness in your mouth, notice these sensations as you breathe. Feel free to give yourself a couple of breaths as you work on noticing the reality of your own experience. Do not be surprised if this one takes a little practice. Be gentle and patient with yourself as you master it.

> "Feelings come and go like clouds in a windy sky. Conscious breathing is my anchor." —Thích Nhất Hạnh, *Stepping into Freedom: Rules of Monastic Practice for Novices*

Step 3: Decide what this moment means now. Make a decision about what your experience points to, right now, without living in the past. Give yourself the chance to make a conscious, informed decision about what is actually taking place in this moment and where it is pointing you next. Step three is important, because it is where you claim an experience as your own and become fully present within it.

> "You have to remember one life, one death—this one! To enter fully the day, the hour, the moment whether it appears as life or death, whether we catch it on the in-breath or out-breath, requires only a moment, this moment." —Stephen Levine, *A Year to Live: How to Live This Year as If It Were Your Last*

These three steps, taken together, begin the process of initiating the mindfulness response.

The mindfulness response is rooted in the principle of assuming responsibility for your own appraisals. Appraisal, in fact is the foundation of everything you learn here.

Practice!

The three steps I have just shared may sound simple. But the truth is, they do take a bit of practice to master and turn into constructive, conscious, and healthy responses when you encounter a potentially stressful situation.

Think back to the example of the automobile with the flat tire from the previous chapter. Look closely at how the three steps I just shared with you could connect with that event.

Initially: We step out of our meeting and notice the car in the parking spot and the flat tire. A neurological storm sweeps through our brain, faster than we could possibly control, and sends a message like, "Why me?" Or: "Who did this to me?" Or: any unproductive question.

Step one: We accept the situation. We do not fight it. We do not deny it. We do not swear at it. We do not scream at it. We just notice our reaction, that it *was* a reaction. Say "yes" to the reality of what is in front of us. It is what is happening; we got a flat tire. That is the reality.

Step two: We breathe and notice. There is nothing mystical or magical about this step. We just take a deep breath and use that breath to *notice* what is happening in our own body and in the sensory messages it is receiving. Is there tightness or discomfort anywhere? Is there tension? Is there some part of our body that feels less relaxed than any other part? Notice it, and experience awareness about what that tension is telling you. Maybe we breathe deep and feel tension in our shoulders as we stare at the flat tire. Maybe the process of noticing that helps the tension in our shoulders to recede.

Step three: We decide what it means now. This is the point where we take conscious control of ourselves and the situation. For instance, we might conclude: "Hey, this kind of thing happens. It's frustrating, but it's not the worst thing that has ever happened to me." Then we might want to ask a good question: "What happens next? I guess

I need to call the people I'm meeting with next and let them know what's happening. Then I can get to work on changing this tire."

This is the mindfulness response.

Beginning with this chapter, I will share brief, simple, *but extremely important* action items that I want you to complete before you move forward in this book. Your assignment for this chapter is to memorize and practice the three steps of the appraisal process and then use it at least once during the course of the next twenty-four hours. When you have done this you will be ready to move on to Chapter Four, which will show you how the mind and the body are connected.

CHAPTER 4

The Mind/Body Continuum

"The mind is like a wild stallion, and you must learn
to tame it."—Anonymous

I HAVE TO PREFACE EVERYTHING IN THIS CHAPTER WITH A
warning. Sometimes people hear me talk about the mind/
body continuum and prejudge what I am about to tell them. They
assume that what I mean is, "Stress is all in your head. If you have
a problem with stress, you only have a psychological problem."
That is not true.

The experience of stress expresses itself in both the mind and
the body. Therefore, a healthy response to stress involves both the
mind and the body. There is a mind/body continuum that experiences
stress.

In addition to emotional responses, such as feeling overwhelmed,
depressed, or even sad, stress can also produce physiological responses
that can adversely affect our health. A researcher by the name of Hans
Seyle developed the General Adaptation Syndrome (GAS) theory
to explain what happens to us on a physiological level when we are

experiencing stress. He identified a three-stage process by which the body responds to stress.

Alarm stage: This is the initial reaction to stress. This stage is marked by activation of the fight-or-flight response, by which the body mobilizes energy necessary to either take part in a physical conflict or flee. The fight/flight response causes intense physiological arousal. Think of the last time you were confronted with fear. Did you experience any type of physiological reaction? My guess would be yes. Our central nervous system becomes activated when triggered by threatening or challenging physical or psychological events. The specific division of the central nervous system I am referring to is the *sympathetic division*. This part of our nervous system increases psychological and physiological arousal and prepares the body for action. This explains why you may experience some physiological responses, such as dryness in the mouth, profuse sweating, increased heart rate, dilated pupils, increased adrenaline activity, and even goose bumps.

Resistance stage: This is the body's reaction to continued stress after the initial spike of the alarm stage. Most of the physiological responses return to normal levels; however, the body used up a great deal of energy. The other subdivision of our central nervous system called the *parasympathetic division* is responsible for returning our body to a calmer state. Your heart rate goes back to normal; you stop sweating; your pupils are constricted; and your adrenaline glands decrease in activity.

Exhaustion stage: This is the body's reaction to long-term, continuous stress. It is marked by degradation of internal organ functions and/or weakening of the immune system.

If you experience chronic stress on a day-to-day basis, this will have a cumulative effect on your psychological as well as physical health. Because of this, healthy stress-management practices are necessary.

When a person does not manage stress effectively, physical symptoms, such as headache, backache, muscle pain, or any number of disorders resulting from compromised organ and immune system function can result. Listed below are commonly reported stress-related physical and behavioral symptoms.

Ten Common Stress-Related Physical Symptoms

- Asthmatic or allergic problems: worsening of problems.
- Eating problems: overeating or under-eating.
- Fatigue: feeling tired or exhausted without excessive physical activity.
- Intestinal difficulties: constipation or diarrhea.
- Heart palpitations.
- Headaches: migraines.
- High blood pressure.
- Hypersomnia: tendency to sleep excessively/ Insomnia: inability to sleep.
- Muscle pain and tension: occurring in neck, shoulders, and back.
- Weakened immune system: more susceptible to a cold, flu, or other medical complications.

It is time for us to look more closely at how the process of mindfulness can serve as the entry point to a constructive response to everyday stress. This will leave us physically and mentally able to cope with life's challenges.

I will begin by sharing a true story about one about my clients, whom I will call Tim.[1] In this first example, I want you to notice how strong the connection was between the stressors in Tim's life and the physical manifestations of his poorly managed reactions to stress.

---

1   Client names represented in this book are pseudonyms to protect confidentiality.

Tim, an assistant bank manager, was having problems with his boss Gerald, who always seemed to be making life difficult. Tim speculated that Gerald was jealous of Tim's ability to manage the bank more effectively. Tim tended to outshine the boss. Who knows whether or not that was actually true?

It is quite normal to experience some kind of conflict in the workplace, and I want to emphasize that there is nothing inherently unhealthy about conflict itself. It is part of how human beings interact and solve problems. The constant tension between Tim and his boss had become a problem for Tim. He was chronically physically sick: he had severe migraine headaches, nausea, and a really overwhelming sense of anxiety whenever he knew he had to go in to work. I want to underline here that Tim's experience was not "all in his head." He really was physically ill, and his illness was directly connected to the high levels of poorly managed stress in his life. In clinical terms, we refer to this as a psychosomatic disorder, where actual physical illness is present as a result of contributing psychological factors.

After Tim told me what he was going through, I said, "Why don't we try this? Ask yourself a question. What is it you're feeling when you wake up, and you know that you have to go to work in the morning?"

He said, "I'm feeling anxiety. I get a headache. In fact, the moment I start thinking about going into work and dealing with Gerald, I get a headache and have stomach problems."

"Okay, what is that all about, do you think?"

"Well I just know he's going to yell at me or tell me I didn't do something right or maybe ridicule me in front of my subordinates."

So I said, "Okay, let's stop right there. How difficult would it be for you to get up in the morning and make a conscious effort to think that it's going to be a good day and that all the positive things in your world are going to unfold? Is it possible for you to envision a day where you have harmonious interactions with your boss and that everything goes smoothly?"

He looked a little surprised, and then he said, "You know, I never even thought of trying to do that. I guess I just got so used to assuming that there were going to be problems that I got into the habit of envisioning how things were going to turn out badly."

I want to be clear here that while "positive thinking" is a good tool, and even an essential tool, it is usually not enough on its own to create a constructive stress-management strategy. Although the advice I gave Tim was a good starting point, I knew that positive imagery alone was not going to be enough to solve his problems. This is one of the reasons I like to assign homework, because it gives people the opportunity to make constructive, active changes to their behavior out in the "real world," and in this case the homework involved a new daily routine: positive affirmations, positive self-thought, and positive visualization.

I assigned Tim a homework assignment. I told him, "For the next week, the minute you wake up, I want you to think about how the day could unfold positively. I want you to do that before you even get out of bed. I want you to create a world in which you don't have any issues with your boss, where communicate effectively with him share a harmonious workplace. Once you are able to see that world, I think you will find it is a bit easier to respond to whatever situation presents itself at work."

Tim agreed to do this.

I said, "If something happens, if your boss engages in those behaviors that make you feel stressed, I want you to do three things. First, just have the intention of looking at the situation in a nonjudgmental manner. Whatever it is, it is neither good nor bad—it is just what it is. Accept that about your boss and about yourself.

"Next, I want you to be aware of what you're personally experiencing regarding that particular situation. What do you see, hear, feel, taste, and smell? Create a point of awareness. Just notice what is going on through your senses. Then respond authentically. Do what feels right to you in the here and now. Just handle this moment that's in front of you with 100 percent attention."

Noticing is not the same as being worried about what you are going to do next or what might happen to you after the discussion, or about what happened last night. It means just being present in this situation and taking action appropriately.

The Mindfulness Response

Look once again at the steps of the mindfulness response. Experience the situation with the intention of looking at it in a nonjudgmental manner. Breathe in, and become aware of what you are personally experiencing. Accept the situation and choose what it means to you, so you can respond authentically—all without judging what is happening.

Mindfulness entails being *present in the moment* without your mind wandering through past events or stories, being *aware* of your physiological responses, and experiencing full *acceptance of the moment* without judging it.

Notice how I offered Tim some tools he could use to move beyond his story about how his boss resented him, always picked on him, wasn't fair, and so on.

> The mindfulness response is an easy point of entry to understanding your situation with clarity.

He said, "Okay, it sounds great, but it sounds like it's going to be very difficult. I can't imagine getting out of the habit of thinking about all the terrible things that may to happen during the day. I guess I built up that routine."

I responded, "Let us take it one step at a time. What if, when you get up in the morning and before you get out of bed, you think about nothing instead of thinking about how things are about to go badly? Start the day with a clean slate focusing on what is happening right then and there."

He said, "Well if I'm not thinking about anything, why am I getting up?"

And I replied, "To enjoy your day."

He agreed to give that a try. He said, "Maybe I'll pretend it's Saturday, imagine that I have time off and I get to spend the morning with my children."

I told him that was a great place to start. The idea was to avoid creating a wave of anxiety first thing in the morning. He was working himself up into a state before he even left the house.

> "Don't believe everything you think. Thoughts are just that thoughts." —Allan Lokos, *Pocket Peace: Effective Practices for Enlightened Living*

Practice enjoying the day.

The next day, Tim woke up and had the intention of enjoying the day. He pretended it was Saturday. When Tim went in to work, it turned out that his boss was late coming in. That was fortunate, because it gave him a chance to go over some of the ideas that we had been talking about in our session and practice using them in other settings.

He had gotten the day off to a good start. He was able to start visualizing positive events. He practiced enjoying the day.

We are often so comfortable thinking about the negative that when I ask clients to think about something positive, just like I asked Tim, they actually have no experience doing that. So of course they will lapse back into their story about how the world is unfair or the boss is jealous, etc.

And by the way, that is not just Tim. That is what most of us tend to do. If we are not careful, we fall into patterns of thinking that we've developed over the years that do not support us. We need to give ourselves time to practice some new patterns. I will discuss this a little later in the book.

Since Tim had some time before the boss got into work, he had a chance to think about how he could respond to his boss in more constructive ways. When the boss finally came in, Tim found that he was surprisingly cordial—not just to Tim but to everybody in the office. He stepped briefly into Tim's office to discuss an account and did not see him again for the rest the day.

The next day, Tim did the exact same thing. He visualized nothing when he got up and focused on pretending it was Saturday and then made his way into work. The boss made it in on time. There were no problems that day.

It kept on that way for about two weeks—no positive interactions, no negative interactions, just neutral—until one day the boss slipped back into a familiar pattern. He started denigrating Tim in front of other people.

I asked Tim, "How did you respond to that?"

Tim said, "Well, you know what? I took my time. I took a deep breath. I thought about those three steps you gave me. I made the intention not to judge what was happening. I noticed what was taking place in my body. Then I thought about what I was going to do. I knew what to do. I moved our conversation over to a place where we could sit down and have a private moment. And I said, 'Look, Gerald, I can't help noticing that sometimes you come off very harsh to me, sometimes even in front of other people. I feel I really don't deserve that.' And I stopped talking. And he just looked at me, and then he nodded."

What I want you to notice here is that by taking a deep breath and hooking into the present moment, Tim was able to avoid replaying old patterns that connected with his previous story. And because he gave the boss a different response, he got a different response in return.

Tim went on: "Gerald said, 'I'm so sorry. I've been experiencing difficult family issues over the past couple of months, and I've been taking things out on you and the staff. I really shouldn't have done that.'"

That response totally changed the relationship, and this wouldn't have happened unless Tim had been able to change his internal approach to the stressful situation. Tim took control of what he noticed and what it meant. Once he did that, the physical symptoms disappeared over time.

He accomplished that with a mindfulness response of *appraisal, awareness,* and a *conscious decision about what it meant in the here and now.* Notice that taking control—responding rather than reacting—starts with learning to notice when you are stressed out.

Here comes your assignment. Before you move on to the next chapter, please complete the worksheet that follows.

Do you know when you're stressed out?

Now that you know that stress can produce real physical symptoms, it is time for you to identify when you are starting to feel overwhelmed by stress before it affects you physically.

I developed the Stress Identification Profile™ (SIP) to help you identify your personal reactions to stress.

To help you get started, use the following material to identify your personal reactions to stress. Please note the items listed below are common responses people report they experience when they are feeling stressed. By no means is this list exhaustive. It is possible that none of these responses may be applicable to you. Therefore, you may have to add in your own responses. Use the SIP indicator to track your personal physiological, emotional, and behavioral responses.

Common Responses to Stress*

Physiological Responses
- Vague physical complaints
- Sweaty palms
- Dilated pupils
- Chest pains
- Trembling
- Digestive problems
- Frequent nausea
- Headaches/backaches
- Frequent colds/flu
- Skin irritation
- Unexplained muscle tension

Emotional
- Disproportionate sadness
- Disproportionate anger
- Disproportionate aggressiveness

- Disproportionate hostility
- Frequent mood swings
- Irritability
- Anxiousness
- Apathy (loss of pleasure)
- Feeling hyper

Behavioral
- Explosive outbursts
- Constant complaining
- Dependence on alcohol/other substances
- Lack of concentration
- Chronic fatigue
- Significant weight gain or loss
- Too much/lack of sleep
- Loss of sex drive
- Cynical or hostile
- Withdrawal/isolation
- Increased self-criticism
- General negative disposition

*Please keep in mind this list is by no means exhaustive.

Stress Identification Profile™

Common Physiological Responses

1. _____
2. _____
3. _____
4. _____
5. _____

Common Emotional Responses

1. _____
2. _____

3. _____
4. _____
5. _____

Common Behavioral Responses

1. _____
2. _____
3. _____
4. _____
5. _____

Chapter 5

Here and Now

"It's good to have an end in mind but in the end what counts is how you travel." —Orna Ross

WHEN TIM USED THE THREE STEPS I HAVE DESCRIBED TO YOU: *appraisal, awareness,* and an authentic *response,* he was using the mindfulness response.

People who are healthy in mind, body, and spirit tend to use the mindfulness response. This is what happy people do, what resourceful people do, and what grateful people do. They use mindfulness to manage both the everyday and major stressors in their lives in a healthy way.

"Life is not about waiting for the storm to pass, it is about learning to dance in the rain." —Vivian Greene

I call this three-step process the mindfulness response, but you can call it whatever makes it easiest for you to start using it. Whatever name you choose to apply to these three steps—presence, engagement, or even prayer—I would like you to notice that it is a resilience strategy that involves mindfulness.

What we are talking about is a pattern of adjustment that involves personal acceptance of the situation you are in and a deliberate response to it instead of simply reacting mindlessly. This is a learned skill that will allow you to take control of the present moment, to reclaim the *here and now!*

In this chapter, we will look at a very basic form of mindfulness response practice, one that most people are comfortable starting with. This practice involves simply noticing stressors during the course of the day and then letting the stress go. In the next chapter, I will share the full mindfulness meditation practice that is the core of this system. By embracing both of these techniques, you will learn the guidelines for developing an individual mindfulness practice that works for you.

Reclaiming Right Now!

Constructive responses to stress require the willingness to step back, look at the *here and now*, and see the glass as half full rather than half empty. Or you could simply see the water in the glass without applying any label whatsoever! The mindfulness response allows you to use this kind of acceptance in the present tense to adjust and deal with the situation you are experiencing. It helps you find a way to acknowledge your situation, to accept and be totally present in it. This takes a little practice.

I find that most of my clients need early support and help with mindfulness in order to create a good initial practice. That is because effective stress management is a matter of changing your patterns of thought and behavior. Specifically, it requires cognitive reappraisal, which is the habit of redefining what a given moment means.

Note that I am not talking about reinforcing the "Pollyanna effect," the tendency to remember pleasant experiences over unpleasant ones. What I am emphasizing is the ability to look at a situation *as it is* and then deal with it consciously and resourcefully. Cognitive reappraisal means taking control of the way you look at a given event. Most of us have decades of less-than-resourceful habits when it comes to how we appraise events in our lives.

Mindfulness is a learned skill and will become habitual over time. A big part of mastering that learned skill is cultivating a simple willingness to step back in any given situation and deal with the facts in a constructive, healthy way.

Here is an example. Let us assume that you are at work, and you receive a text message telling you that your daughter has been in an auto accident. She has no injuries, and neither does the other driver, but the car has been totaled. She is dealing with the police and will call you as soon as she can.

Initially, you may experience a rush of physiological symptoms, such as sweaty palms, nausea, or even heart palpitations. That reaction is both natural and understandable. Once you let that initial reaction pass, you are going to want to have a discussion with yourself about what is actually going on.

Your first instinct might be to ride that wave of adrenaline, and even intensify it, by saying something like, "I'm so upset with her. I told her not to drive on that road at night; she never listens to me." Your job is to appraise, become aware, then respond to the event.

You might ask yourself: "Is that really what's happening?"

Your job is to clear your mind and think about the facts and what they really mean. After all, you are the one who imparts meaning to the facts you identify. You are the one who chooses what words to speak and what thoughts to follow.

Honoring the here and now means learning to grow our own thoughts and then accept personal responsibility for planting them.

We have roughly sixty thousand thoughts a day. The question I am asking here is: How consciously are we managing our thought processes? Are we taming our minds? Are we allowing or minds to run wild? Or are we throwing ourselves into a river of anxiety and drama? Our goal is to be in control of our thoughts so we can make conscious and healthy decisions.

So let us go back to the situation where you receive that difficult message about the car accident. You have already told yourself a story about what has happened. Maybe you did not realize it at first, but you can realize it now! What did you tell yourself? "My daughter was driving on the road I warned her to avoid!" Do you know for certain that she was driving on the road you told her to avoid? If not, you can exclude that as a fact.

Similarly, do you know for certain that she "never" listens to your advice? Even if it is tempting to answer yes, you can choose to save that statement for later. Do not treat that as a fact right now. Stick to what you know for sure, which is that she has been an accident, and she is fine. With this in mind, you can respond consciously instead of reacting instinctively.

When we first encounter new stressors we are often in reaction mode. We are not responding consciously. Unlike a conscious response, reacting adds a lot of emotion and a lot of stories. That is understandable, because we have been conditioned to react rather than to respond to situations. However, it is not the best way to move forward. If you are distracted by a surge of emotions about something that has no factual relevance to the situation, that distraction is going to affect your cognitive processing, and you are going to have trouble dealing constructively with the situation at hand.

Practice stepping back and saying to yourself, "These are the facts. This is what I know for sure. How should I assess this situation? What needs to be done next?" Only when you have a clear understanding of what is actually happening can you then decide how to effectively deal with the situation. You may also find lessons learned or takeaways regarding your situation. For example, you might choose to be grateful for the fact that no one was injured. You might conclude that now your daughter has had this experience, she is more likely to become a more conscientious driver.

Or perhaps in previous months you felt some distance between you and your daughter, and now, in a crisis, you have a chance to come together and get a lot closer.

With persistence and practice, you can find a way to incorporate positive, constructive avenues of meaning into just about any potentially stressful situation. If you happen to notice yourself holding onto a particular interpretation of events that does not fit the facts you can confirm, it is possible that you are holding on to some past, unresolved events. At this point you may want to stop and ask yourself: "Why am I interpreting events in this way?"

> "We do not let go in order to make ourselves impoverished or bereft. We let go in order to discover happiness and peace."—Christina Feldman

It Only Takes a Moment

My point here is *not* that you should spend all day analyzing the stressors in your life. Appraisal should be a brisk, forward-moving process. It should be something you work on every day. It takes just a moment.

This is what I share with my clients about cognitive reappraisal. This is a skill you need to learn through practice. It should become a tool for managing the day. It is not something that takes place once a week when we get together for a counseling session. I am not going to be there with you during the course of each day. You can simplify the mindfulness response by getting into the habit of asking yourself questions such as:

- What's really happening here?
- What does that mean?
- What needs to happen next?

No matter how experienced we may become, we will always benefit from a little more practice in making constructive assessments about the here and now. My objectives are to help you create and sustain a habit of practicing mindful questioning and to evaluate the here and now constructively. The following exercise can help.

Before you move on to the next chapter, post these questions in a place where you will see them at least three times a day.

- What's really happening here?
- What does that mean?
- What needs to happen next?

CHAPTER 6

Mindfulness Meditation

"When my house burned down I gained an unobstructed view of the moonlight sky." —Zen

*I*F YOU CHANGE ONLY ONE THING IN YOUR LIFE AS A RESULT of reading this book, I hope it will be the act of incorporating just a few minutes of meditation, preferably ten, into your daily routine. Another good name for this activity is "mind-clearing," because it allows you to clear your mind of thoughts. That is really what you are doing: clearing your mind from the thousands of thoughts that are incessantly entering your mind during the day. Just as your body needs to relax, so does your mind.

If you feel that ten minutes a day is too much time to dedicate to this practice that is fine. This is often a challenge that most neophytes experience when they engage in mindfulness meditation. As you become more familiar with the process, you will probably want to expand your meditation time.

What I am talking about is not a huge time commitment. I am talking about devoting just a few minutes a day to doing nothing and thinking about nothing ... to simply being present. It takes just a little practice to establish that routine, and I will help you do so in this chapter.

Why should we make such an effort? Why should we bother to learn how to be present in those ten minutes? Because our lives have become so distracted that we are no longer present in the world. We are human doings instead of human beings.

Investing just a little time each day in meditation can give you a whole new perspective and can leave you with a powerful feeling of being truly present in your own life.

> "Do every act of your life as though it were the very last act of your life." —Marcus Aurelius, *Meditations*

Meditation is not preventive medicine or a panacea. It helps us to get better at being present. Being present is the opposite of having your mind taken over by a half-dozen different things at once.

Meditation offers you the opportunity to familiarize yourself with the present moment and focus. It allows you to see your thoughts and experience your emotions as they come and go. Think of emotions as a wave in the ocean. A wave comes. A wave collapses. A wave goes. Then another wave comes.

We cannot change everything we might wish to change in our lives, but through meditation we can learn to accept our experiences and perceive events differently. If you think that is worth ten minutes a day, please keep reading!

Where to Start

I am often asked: "How can I learn to meditate? I sit there and sit there, and nothing happens. Am I doing it wrong?"

Or: "What is the secret to meditating?"

Or: "Some people are good at this, but I'm not one of them. How can I make it happen for me?"

It is actually pretty easy to get started with a simple meditation technique. Here are the steps:

Begin by sitting comfortably in a place where all possible distractions have been removed.

- No phones.
- No computers.
- No text messages.
- No TV.
- No music.

Simply sit comfortably and put your body at ease and relax. Follow your breath. Allow your mind to go thoughtless. If a thought comes along, do not worry about it. Let it go. Just keep returning to job one, which is to relax. Some people find it helpful to focus on the breath, while others say that focusing on the breath or anything else is still an activity of the mind.

My experience with my clients is that people generally need a little more guidance in order to benefit from meditation practice. Here is some additional help you begin to establish your routine.

The pose. No, you do not have to learn some complex downward dog yoga pose. No, your thigh does not need to be wrapped around your neck. Sit upright. If you are sitting on the floor, sit cross-legged with your back straight and shoulders down. If you are sitting in a chair, do the same except for the part about crossing your legs. However you sit, it is important that you sit comfortably and remain undisturbed.

The breath. Relax your jaw, relax your tongue, and relax your facial muscles. Slowly inhale through your nostrils and exhale through your mouth. As you are inhaling, think of yourself as filling your lungs with fresh air. Feel your lungs expand. As you exhale through your mouth, envision yourself releasing that air into the world. Constantly be aware of your inhalations and exhalations.

Focus. This is where people usually need a little help. How do you keep your mind from wandering, tossing, and turning over every little thing you need to do later instead of being present in this moment? Some people suggest focusing on one object, such as a candle flame. Others will tell you to focus on your breathing, and still others will suggest that you focus on nothing at all. Try all of these, and see what works for you. The goal is to allow your mind and body to simply relax. Let those random thoughts simply pass by. I like to equate these thoughts with slow moving clouds. Think of clouds moving slowly in the sky. You are not sticking with any cloud, not interpreting or analyzing any cloud, just allowing these clouds to simply pass by. Try this with your thoughts. Allow them to be thoughts that just pass by. Do not assign any significance to them. Do not fight them. If it helps you to focus on your breathing, go back to focusing on the inhalation and exhalation.

Try not to judge yourself. Initially, you may not be able to control thoughts that enter your mind. Just be present in the moment, and focus your mind on seeing these thoughts as distant, as passing in time.

To mantra or not to mantra. That is the question! Meditation is a process. If at first you are finding that you are unable to get into a comfortable pose, breathe properly, or stay focused, do not give up. This is a trial-and-error process. There is no single right way to do it, and no homework or special preparation is required to get started. Some people have found the best way to stay focused is by repeating a word (or even a special phrase), either silently or aloud. Others have found that this repetition tends to distract their focus. Exploring which will work for you is going to take time. My suggestion is to try both and see which approach brings the best results.

Think of this activity as giving yourself a time-out. The idea of relaxing the body and silencing the mind has been associated with many benefits to health and well-being.

As you become comfortable with the process, you may decide that you want to gradually increase your meditation time. Start with at least five minutes a day, and experiment to find what works best for you. Your goal should be a daily meditation practice of at least twenty minutes. Your mind and body will thank you!

Working your way up to meditating for at least twenty minutes a day has been shown to increase productivity, improve relationships with others, and enhance overall health and well-being. If you are new at this, start small. Most of my clients find they are able to commit to ten minutes a day at the outset. Allow me to share a brief example of how meditation practice helped a client of mine to gain clarity and awareness.

A client came to see me, because she was struggling with a great deal of tension, stress, and conflict in her daily life. Financial hardship, an alcoholic and abusive partner, and an unruly stepson led her to seek my services. She said to me, "All I want is some peace in my life." After a few sessions of sorting out her situation, I gave her some instructions about mind-clearing. She went home to practice only to return to my office a week later even more distressed. She spoke of how her mind began to calm down, and she started gaining insight. She became even more acutely aware of the nature of the conflicts in her life and what she needed to do to bring change to her life. Bemused, I asked her what the problem was. She responded, "I did not ask for awareness. I only wanted peace."

Going Outside Your Comfort Zone

When it comes to responding effectively to daily stress, it is important to establish a good daily meditation practice. The following story will help illustrate how big a difference it can make.

Jackie was a pediatric nurse who had been severely abused by her mother as a child. She bore many scars, both physically and psychologically. She was effective at her job; however, she did have severe socialization issues, which caused her to be deeply unhappy in both her personal and professional life.

She came to me, because she had literally no social network, no friends, no significant other, and was deeply withdrawn. She had no strong connections at work and seemed paralyzed with fear at the prospect of developing any genuine connections with her coworkers. Her connections with people were usually superficial.

This client had some serve trauma issues she needed to work through. We spent a great deal of time focusing on her past trauma and helping her to acknowledge and cope with what had happened to her as child. In conjunction with a cognitive-behavioral approach, I integrated mindfulness training, which yielded the following results.

I shared with Jackie the meditation strategies I outlined in beginning of this chapter. Jackie began with only three minutes of meditation a day and worked her way up.

We also used cognitive restructuring, meaning I was able to help her shift negative thinking to more neutral or positive thinking. These two approaches helped her to process her past trauma. I also encouraged her to step outside her comfort zone as a way to lessen her social anxiety and develop a social support system.

I do not want to give the impression that meditation served as some kind of magic wand that instantly made Jackie's life more open to the possibilities of friendships and social support. Meditation served as an ancillary to the therapeutic process. This was a persistent, ongoing process, and it took a great deal of work. But it did deliver a healthy outcome.

Homework Assignment

One of the early activities I asked Jackie to focus on was the possibility of making cupcakes—she prided herself on being an excellent baker. I suggested she bake some cupcakes to share with her colleagues. It took me four sessions to get her to accept the possibility of bringing those cupcakes in to work. Why a cupcake baking assignment? This assignment served as a point of entry for Jackie to engage in something she enjoyed doing; it allowed her a comfortable and safe platform to engage in socializing with her coworkers; and it instilled self-confidence. When she was younger, her mother ridiculed her and at times physically abused her when she did not perform a specific task as requested.

To guide her through this process, we had to develop a hierarchy list ranging from one to ten. Ten was the most stressful part of the cupcake baking assignment. One was the least stressful part of the assignment. She needed visual aide, so we constructed a paper and ink display of worst-case outcomes connected to whatever socialization activity we were considering. In this case, the least worst-case outcome, which went at the bottom of the list, was that she would have to go to the store and get the ingredients for making cupcakes. At the top of the list was the possibility her coworkers might not enjoy her cupcakes and ridicule her. Seeing this visual display made it easier for her to move forward.

A combination of strategies allowed Jackie to establish meaningful friendships at work. By the end of our time together, she was meditating for a full half hour every morning. I do not believe she could have made the behavioral changes she did without the combination of meditation and a supportive therapeutic environment. She was a much happier person when she embraced the daily routine of mindfulness meditation and thus developed a stronger support system with her coworkers. Her anxiety diminished markedly.

As you read this, you may think that your situation is fundamentally different from Jackie's. In fact, I would argue that your situation is essentially identical to hers. She needed to move outside her comfort zone and respond resourcefully to a stressful, anxiety-prone situation, and a daily regimen of meditation helped her to do that. We are often immobilized by our situation, because of our inability to step outside of our comfort zone.

If something simple as a three-minute daily time investment could help Jackie to overcome a challenge as severe as the one she faced, how much could you accomplish in your life by devoting ten minutes today to your own inner happiness?

Before you move on to the next chapter, devote just a few minutes to a meditation session. Set a timer or an alarm clock for five minutes. See how it goes.

You might begin by trying for five minutes. If that proves difficult for you, begin with three minutes. Each day, gradually increase the time by two minutes until you have reached at least ten minutes of daily practice.

Do not proceed to Chapter Seven until you have completed at least one meditation practice.

Chapter 7

Is Your Story Telling You?

MICHAEL, A CLIENT OF MINE, CAME TO SEE ME, BECAUSE HE was having difficulty resolving what his wife's occasional tardiness meant.

Michael's wife Patty was one of those people who, despite her best efforts, seems to run fifteen to forty-five minutes late for just about everything. There was not anything sinister about any of these delays, at least not as far as I could tell, and I spent quite a lot of time communicating with Michael and Patty separately about their relationship. Patty had suggested that Michael come in to see me. This is often how it works: someone in a client's life suggests that he or she seek help in dealing with stress.

What was the real issue? It turned out that just about every time Patty returned late from shopping or a visit with a girlfriend, Michael went into paroxysms of doubt, jealousy, and barely suppressed rage concerning her whereabouts. He was convinced she was having an affair.

> Michael's knee-jerk response to Patty's occasional lateness was to accuse her of having an affair.

Sometimes he was able to conceal these emotions, and sometimes he wasn't.

When he did manage to conceal them, he told me he was left feeling overwhelmed and exhausted. Expressing them brought Patty to (in her words) her "wit's end."

The two had been married for nearly three years, and on virtually every occasion Patty had been late to return from some errand or one of her social events, which occurred infrequently, Michael created a catastrophic explanation for her tardiness. In his worst moments, he was completely convinced that she was seeing another man and believed she was guilty until proven innocent.

I have used the word "convinced," but actually that implies more rational thought than actually existed in any of these situations. Michael really had no evidence whatsoever to suggest that there were such serious problems in the relationship, and he had no credible reason to suspect Patty. But he still found himself deeply concerned about what seemed to him to be the reality of her infidelity.

I listened carefully as both parties explained the situation. Each offered a personal perspective. Patty came across as someone who wanted to fix a problem rather than someone who wanted to escape one. She told me she was not having an affair, and I believed her. Yet Michael was committed, with deep certainty and with strong emotion, to the explanation he had created for himself.

Please understand what we are talking about are occasional, benign episodes of lateness, not a daily pattern, and not any kind of subterfuge in any other area of married life. In the period between the time when Patty was supposed to arrive home from a shopping trip and the time she actually arrived home, whether that period was five minutes or forty-five minutes, Michael filled his mind with dark, disturbing, and painful fantasies about what he imagined Patty was doing behind his back with another man.

It did not take me long to figure out that this was a serious challenge for the relationship. No amount of proof or outside corroboration seemed capable of changing Michael's thought process while waiting for Patty. When she arrived late, he was overtaken by a curiosity to confront her, to make her prove that she had not betrayed him. Sometimes he fought this curiosity. Other times he could not.

What was happening here?

The Story

Michael had a story. It was a story he had grown accustomed to telling himself, accustomed to using to help him deal with various stressful situations in his life. He had a lot of past experiences with this story. Very often the story worked in the sense that it helped Michael to make sense of his surroundings. This is usually the case for most people. We often use past stories and experiences to help us understand our current situation.

I mention this because I do not want to leave the impression that Michael's situation was notable primarily because of how different it was from everyone else's. Michael's story reached a point where its *consequences* were unmanageable, a point where it was no longer an effective tool for interacting with stressors in his life. It created more stress—both for him and for Patty.

Michael's story sounded like this: *If I can convince you that you let me down, then you will love me.*

It is not so much that Michael was telling himself this story. The story was telling him! It was dictating what Patty's occasional episodes of tardiness *meant*. It was interesting to me that no amount of conscientious updating from Patty by phone regarding her whereabouts could alter this story of Michael's. It was deeply ingrained. It had been there for years. It would take work to dislodge.

Now, if we wanted to, we could spend pages and pages in this book evaluating exactly where this story came from. (It originated, I learned, in Michael's relationship with his mother.)

However, I do not want to spend a great deal of time analyzing where this particular story came from, and there are two very good reasons for this. First, I have found that such explanations might give you the impression that if you didn't happen to have the same early-life circumstances that Michael did, you don't have a story, and that is certainly not true. In my experience, we *all* have stories that we use to deal with stressful situations, and some of those stories leave us less resourceful than we need to be. If we follow the "reasoning" of these stories, we will find ourselves catastrophizing and reacting, just as Michael was doing, rather than disengaging and responding consciously.

Second, going into all the details of the origins of Michael's story might lead you to believe that the best way to deal with a similar story—a story that is standing in the way of a healthy response to stress—is to spend months or years re-experiencing your past, either on your own or with a therapist. That's not true, unless you are experiencing some major adjustment difficulties, and Michael was not. The best approach, in my experience, is a much more direct, pragmatic discussion that leads to this question: *How can I learn to notice this story when it presents itself so I can move beyond it when I decide for myself that it doesn't fit the circumstances?*

Appraisal

Before I go into the specifics of how I helped Michael learn to get his footing during those difficult times, I want to ask you to think of a time when you might have applied a similar story to a stressful situation in your own life.

In all likelihood, your story sounded different from Michael's. Perhaps you found yourself creating an obstacle in a friendship by playing the victim. *When I act like I'm abandoned, people will support me.*

Or perhaps you found a way to get out of a difficult situation at work by insisting loudly and repeatedly that you were right, even though the facts might not have completely supported you. *If I intimidate you, I win.*

Or maybe there was an entirely different story in play. These stories are default coping strategies for dealing with stressful realities. They are in all likelihood just as deeply ingrained in your life as Michael's was ingrained in his. Of course, I do not know what your story is, because I have never explored that issue with you. I can assure you that Michael's story, limiting and extremely painful as it was, represents hundreds of non-resourceful coping stories that I have encountered in other clients and in everyday life.

Just about everyone has the opportunity to come to terms with the limitations of this kind of story at one point or another. I urge you to read what follows not as though Michael were some special case but as though you were standing in for him. In all likelihood, only the details of the story and the event that triggers it are different from your situation.

I worked one-on-one with Michael for multiple sessions, and after three of those sessions he agreed with my suggestion that what we really needed to do was help him to learn to appraise his story differently. I wanted him to identify what about the story was actually relevant.

Michael agreed that when he found himself doubting his wife's faithfulness, he would try to stop what he was doing, change his breathing pattern, and ask himself certain questions about the situation he was facing. These questions included:

Have I ever had any indication that Patty was unfaithful to me in the past?

Has Patty ever lied to me about where she actually was when she was late?

Has Patty kept her agreement about keeping me informed concerning when she's going to be late and why?

In addition to the questions that you just read, I also persuaded Michael to engage in a daily routine of meditation (or mind-clearing) exercise for ten minutes a day. I believe that had a positive impact on his ability to step back from the situation and pose constructive questions for himself.

By suggesting that Michael learn to pose better questions about the situations he was facing, I helped him get a clearer sense of his story, and I helped him to notice how relevant or useful that story was (or wasn't) in his current situation. I was not discounting events that happened to him in the past with other people. I was only saying to him that in terms of formulating a constructive response to a minor stressor situation (his work situation), his story might not be all that useful. If he examined it and decided that for himself, he might eventually decide to let go of it.

And that is exactly what happened. Michael agreed to take a deep breath and appraise his own reactions, gauge their relevance to his situation, and decide on his own about how accurately they described his world. After about three months of attentive practice he had moved beyond the negative, debilitating feelings of betrayal. He was able to have better, constructive conversations with Patty. He also began to notice other events in his life where the story surfaced as an explanation for the "disloyal" behavior of friends or colleagues. In time, he also learned how to put these situations into perspective and step away from them.

Notice Your Story

For Michael and for all of us, a critical early step is to notice the story. Sometimes this will require the assistance of a trained person who can help you to notice and evaluate your story.

There is tremendous power,

What I would like you to do before you move on to the next chapter is identify at least one limiting story that you have used to cope with a stressful situation. Identifying that story allows you to examine if that story is working for you.

authenticity, and integrity in learning to recognize and assess your own story. Very often, we find that a single, one-size-fits-all explanation for problems in relationships or circumstances beyond our control has become ingrained. We may even find that the story has become our "default setting" for interacting with the world and that it is no longer supporting us. Just as Michael did, we can learn to make our own decisions about whether or not the story is really all that relevant to what we're facing in the here and now.

CHAPTER 8

Handling the Everyday Hassles of Life

"In the end, just three things matter:
How well we have lived.
How well we have loved.
How well we have learned to let go."
—Jack Kornfield

IN THIS CHAPTER, I SHARE THREE POWERFUL STORIES BASED on my work with clients who learned to handle what I have called the "everyday hassles of life." As you will recall, these hassles are also known as minor stressors.

All the stories are composites, meaning that they combine elements of multiple clients I have worked with over time. This was necessary in order to protect my clients' confidentiality. The cases in question involved sensitive personal information that had to be altered to avoid identifying a particular client.

All three stories capture the essence of the success stories they embodied. These cases offer important insights on the best ways to put the principles I have shared in this book into practical application.

Lisa's Story

Lisa, a young copyeditor, had been fired from three different publishing jobs over the course of twenty-four months. She had earned a reputation as someone who was "difficult to work with." She was brilliant and quite good at what she did, but she was out of work now and having major trouble reclaiming her once-promising career trajectory, because past employers could not be persuaded to give her good recommendations. Her job search in a highly competitive industry was not going well.

In addition, her personal relationships were failing. There were deep grudges with several of her close family members, and she reported that she was experiencing major problems with her boyfriend. It was at her boyfriend's request that she came to see me. The two of them attended their sessions together, which made this couple's therapy.

When I asked Lisa to explain the kinds of problems she felt she was having, she said, "People are hypersensitive, and I sometimes have trouble communicating with hypersensitive people." There is a lot I could share with you about the dynamics of this couple's relationship, but since we are focusing on Lisa, I will give you the bare facts of the typical situations that would set her off into a cycle of catastrophizing.

Early on in our discussion, I asked Lisa to explain what the "hypersensitivity" issue in their relationship looked like from her point of view.

"He'll freeze me out," Lisa said. "I'll do something he doesn't like, but he'll overreact. To start with, he won't tell me what the problem is. It's like pulling teeth to get him to talk sometimes. I know full well that something's wrong. But when I ask him to tell me what's wrong, he gets all defensive."

Bob had a very different take on what was happening in their relationship. According to him, Lisa often pressed him for solutions to problems when there were not any problems to solve.

It was true, he said, that he sometimes had to "let things cook" for a while, and often, he needed a couple of hours to figure out exactly what was bothering him about an exchange with Lisa. When he did identify the issue, he was more than happy to talk about it.

The real challenge was that Bob just did not like talking as much as Lisa did, particularly at the end of a weekday. According to Bob, he talked all day at work. He was not up for more talking when he made it home.

Like a lot of men, Bob felt comfortable with long stretches of silence once he reached a point of being "talked out." Lisa, however, did not feel as comfortable with these silences as Bob did. Often, Lisa interpreted Bob's silence as a judgment or even an attack on her.

According to Bob, the majority of their conflicts arose from Lisa's inability to accept that he was not much of a conversationalist at the end of a long work day. "If there's a problem, and if I know what it is," he said, "I'll talk it over with her. But if there isn't a problem, she pushes and nags me until that becomes the problem."

I asked Lisa to tell me what kinds of hypersensitivity issues she had experienced in the workplace. She told me of Juan, a colleague with whom she had difficulties. She insisted she had observed Juan, a fellow editor, staring her down.

Just as Bob's silences did, Juan's "staring" set off a negative cycle. According to Lisa, Juan became "touchy" when she approached him about his way of looking at her.

I asked Lisa to tell me what kind of communication style she used to discuss this with Juan. She began the conversation with these words, "What's your problem?" Not exactly the best way to start a conversation with a coworker.

We spent some time examining what was happening in each

of these situations. Fortunately, the rapport we established at the beginning of our session was quite good, and Lisa was genuinely interested in getting to the bottom of these difficult interactions at home and work. She was open to discussing how she might be making things more difficult than they had to be for herself and others.

Here is what that discussion revealed: When people who were important to Lisa presented her with silence or with looks that could be construed as disapproving, Lisa went on the attack. This happened with her siblings as well. Why? Well, it turns out that over several years, Lisa had developed a narrative that went something like this: *If you're not with me, you're against me.*

How did that narrative develop? Further examination led us to the discovery that this story arose from Lisa's interactions with her father. The narrative had a great deal to do with the fact that Lisa grew up in a household that had some major substance abuse problems. Her father alternated between periods of abusive behavior and catatonic silence. For our purposes here, the details of these issues are not that important. What matters is that Lisa was able to recognize where the *if you're not with me, you're against me* narrative came from. Eventually, she was also able to recognize that while that particular narrative had been instrumental in allowing her to survive a traumatic family situation, it was not serving her well in her current situation.

When Lisa heard silence from Bob, she automatically translated the silence as, "Bob is no longer in love with me." Obviously, that was a scary proposition. So she went into action: *If you're not with me, you're against me.*

When Lisa saw a strange expression on Juan's face, she automatically translated that expression as "Juan is out to get me." Once again, she locked into the, *if you're not with me, you're against me* narrative. If there was going to be a fight, she was going to be the one who came out on top!

Lisa's narrative led her to assume that there was a problem ... and it also led her to assume that she was at the center of that problem.

Lisa's turnaround did not take place overnight, and it was not the kind of change that instantly transformed all of her exchanges with the important people in her life. But it was a dramatic turnaround all the same. Here is how we moved forward.

We discussed the negative cycle at length. This took multiple sessions, but Lisa eventually came to accept—on her own—that she sometimes unintentionally engaged in a hair-trigger, best-offense-is-a-good-defense maneuver. This was a reaction, not a response. She noticed that the knee-jerk reaction was completely irrelevant to what was really happening in front of her. Silence did not necessarily mean her relationship was in trouble. A coworker who looked at her might be admiring her clothing and not provoking an attack. I want to emphasize that these, too, were conclusions that Lisa reached on her own. They did not materialize overnight, but they did emerge after extensive examination, guidance, and support.

I gave Lisa homework assignments. This involved journaling, cognitive reappraisal, and mind-clearing exercises.

Lisa got better at noticing when she was reacting to a situation instead of responding to it. That does not mean she always responded consciously to situations that triggered her narrative, and it certainly does not mean the narrative went away. It does mean she became more effective at spotting it when it presented itself. Once she learned to spot it, she could practice stepping back.

By the time we had completed our sessions, Lisa had started a successful freelance editing business. She had also improved her relationship with Bob, and the two are still together and happy.

Frank's Story

Frank was a high-powered senior marketing executive who had spent many years at one of the company's prestigious consumer product firms. At one time, he had been on the leadership track and had been groomed to become CEO of the company. However, over the last five years, his career and his personal life had taken a sharp turn for the worse.

His attention to detail, which had once been his hallmark, had begun to slip. He had begun to miss important meetings, and he had nearly gotten the company in trouble with a series of unfortunate remarks at an office party that many people in attendance had construed as sexist. Only some deft diplomacy from the CEO had headed off a lawsuit.

Frank's appearance was no longer sharp, and the top-notch suits he once wore had given way to whatever he could manage to find in the closet. When I first met him, I remember thinking that he was a strangely rumpled-looking senior corporate executive.

It became clear to me both from Frank's remarks in our early sessions and from the e-mail I had received from his CEO, that there were some patterns of behavior here that merited close examination. His staff consisted mainly of women, and he seemed to spend more and more of his working day enraged at their seemingly constant errors. If you had asked him what the problem was (and I did), he would have told you that the problem was the incompetence of people he had been unwise enough to hire—all of whom happened to be women.

Frank's professional relationships with female colleagues, which had never been good, had in recent years become openly antagonistic. His working relationships with his all-female clerical staff had become icy and strained.

Our sessions revealed something else of interest: Frank's personal life was in shambles. No love relationships seemed to matter very much to him, and these relationships now seemed to last a matter of months rather than the three to four years he had been able to sustain in the past.

There did not appear to be a single incident that had triggered Frank's downhill slide. It seemed to be the culmination of a long-simmering descent that affected his social skills. They were abysmal, and they were getting worse. Of course, rudeness or even antisocial behavior is not unheard of among top executives, but in Frank's case his poor interactions with others correlated with an accelerating collapse in his own productivity. He came to see me because the CEO of his firm informed him that if he did not seek help, he would be let go. We worked together under the convenient catch-all heading of "executive coaching." I sensed that he knew he had to take my coaching seriously if he wanted to keep his job, which he did.

Frank and I had generally productive, never-boring sessions for a number of months. He was not an easy person to get along with. It became obvious to me almost instantly that he had a narrative that did not support him. This particular narrative, which I would summarize as *I matter and you don't*, was particularly evident in his relationships with women.

I think the only reason I was able to work with Frank was that I promised him he would not have to lie down on the couch, tell me his life story, and submit to being psychoanalyzed. I was true to my word. However, as the sessions moved forward, it became clear that his attitude toward women, which was profoundly hostile and verging on abusive, did not emerge out of nowhere. It had a history, and when he felt comfortable enough to share it with me, he did.

Frank had been raised by a single mother who was unable to provide him with the attention and love that he deserved. Something happened in his life that happens to a lot of people in Frank's situation. On a verbal level, he expressed love for and even idolized his mother. But underneath, he nursed a deep loathing of his mother, a loathing that could not be expressed directly. So he expressed that hatred in his relations with other women. He was particularly brutal toward women who reported to him professionally. Let me emphasize that we did not spend weeks and weeks replaying and reliving this backstory, but it did emerge and offered some important context. Frank eventually acknowledged its significance.

A deepening, unresolved hostility toward women was a kind of tumor that was consuming Frank's career. I was surprised to learn that he did not even know (or at least claimed not to know) the names of the women who reported to him at work. It was always, "The blonde secretary forgot such-and-such," or "The brunette secretary overlooked so-and-so." They were always letting him down, always making mistakes, and always sabotaging him. During our first few sessions, he never called these women by their names. As far as Frank was concerned, the stress in his life arose from their incompetence.

I could tell that a big part of the real problem was Frank's refusal to acknowledge the way he was interacting with these individuals. He treated these women like dirt. Not surprisingly, this disrespect and aggressive behavior manifested in our relationship. There were many times when he showed up late, or not at all, and had no good reason for doing so.

Frank had established a cycle under which his professional relationships, particularly his professional relationships with women, were based on an ever-deepening hostility and aggression. This, we learned, was because of his early experiences with his own mother. He wanted nurturing and support from women, but since he had not received that as a child, he was afraid to express that desire for support, because he feared that women, like his mother, would reject him. More importantly, he never learned how to ask for the love and nurturing that he so wanted. His feelings of wanting to be close were transformed into resentment, aggression, and even hatred— all in order to protect himself. This all came out indirectly, during conversations about other things and not because I was spending session after session with the sole aim of trying to get to the bottom of his early childhood history. While I am not negating the importance of early childhood experiences for this particular case, it was more important for the client to understand where these feelings originated from and then to help him move forward toward a healthier way of relating to others.

Frank's tendency to degrade and humiliate women who reported to him had only become more pronounced as his career moved forward, and it had left him depleted both personally and professionally. The problem was only getting worse. And now it was threatening his career.

Frank's narrative led him to blame and punish every woman in his life in order to prove that he had power, that he mattered, and that he could not be hurt.

Frank's turnaround was based on the fact that at the end of the day, he really was capable of empathy. He was moved by stories of homeless children, for instance, and he gave generously to charities designed to help them. Here is how we moved forward to expand that empathy.

We discussed the negative cycle at length. This took multiple sessions, but Frank eventually came to accept—on his own—that he sometimes engaged in displays of aggression intended to diminish other people. These displays of aggression hurt people, and he came to acknowledge and regret that. The aggression was a reaction, not a response. An aha moment came when he recognized that intimidating other people did not actually make him more powerful within the hierarchy of the company: it only made him less powerful. In fact, this behavior pattern was about to cost him his job. Through support and guidance, Frank gained insight about his interpersonal style of relating to others.

I gave Frank homework assignments. This involved meditation/ mind-clearing and journaling. Additionally, I asked him to find one positive, constructive comment for the women in his office. Over a week's time, I wanted him to provide each woman in his office with some type of positive, constructive feedback and to refer to them by their names.

Frank got better at noticing when he was reacting to a situation instead of responding to it. By means of extensive role-playing he became more effective at spotting the I matter and you don't narrative. He used role-plays with me to practice interacting with coworkers as human beings, not objects. Eventually, he got pretty good at stepping back from his story.

By the time we completed our sessions, Frank had transformed his relationships with his coworkers and saved his job. He started having significant relationships with women as opposed to the superficial, ephemeral relationships he'd had in the past.

Betty's Story

Betty worked as an executive assistant to a prominent, well-paid criminal defense attorney. Indeed, her job was very demanding. It included many interactions with attorneys working under intense pressure as well as occasional contact with representatives of the court, the press, and members of the law enforcement community. She worked long hours, usually twelve or thirteen hours a day.

When I met Betty, she was in her early forties and had recently married. She had other relationships in the past but had postponed marriage for many years, choosing to put work first in her life. Now she was eager to make her marriage work. She no longer wanted to be alone as she approached late adulthood.

Both professionally and personally, Betty felt overwhelmed. She was usually exhausted from the long hours she worked. A series of bitter fights erupted between her and her new husband over his excessive drinking. This had left the new bride feeling out of control and deeply disillusioned about what her marriage really meant. She had been aware of her partner's drinking before marriage, but she had overlooked it on the theory that she could "work something out" after they married.

Betty came to me because of a physical problem. Her doctor had diagnosed her with irritable bowel syndrome and suspected that its onset might have been stress-related or psychosomatic, which it was.

Betty was a bright, resourceful, ambitious woman who was drowning in a sea of reactive stress patterns. She had a narrative that I would describe as: *I will sacrifice myself for you, and you will love me.* Our sessions together revealed that the genesis of this personal story lay in her relationship with her parents. Betty was the oldest sibling in a family whose disabled mother required constant care. She died when Betty was still a teenager. I share this with you not because it was something Betty had to "relive" or "experience," but because it provided the framework for her breakthrough.

Betty's narrative led her to overcommit because she believed that taking care of others would lead to her feel needed, wanted, and loved.

Betty's turnaround was based on two realizations: that her physical ailment was stress-related and that she was not going to be able to help herself or anyone else if she was unable to establish a better sense of balance in her life. Here is how we moved forward to act on that aha moment.

We discussed the negative cycle at length. The turning point for Betty came when she realized that her altruistic behavior was not only making her ill but also making it impossible for her to move forward toward her own personal and professional goals. She wanted to be an attorney, and she wanted to be in a stable, healthy, and permanent relationship. As it stood, she was not moving any closer to either of those goals. Her knee-jerk willingness to commit herself to others was a reaction not a response. Usually, Betty noticed, the automatic *I will sacrifice myself for you, and you will love me* reaction arose from a misguided belief that her sacrifices would win her appreciation and support, personally and professionally. They did not. Notice again that these were insights that Betty had to reach on her own. I supported her, but she did the work that allowed her to internalize this important lesson.

I gave Betty homework exercises, which consisted of meditation, journaling, and cognitive reappraisal. Betty got better at noticing when she was reacting to a situation instead of responding to it. She became more effective at spotting the *I will sacrifice myself for you, and you will love me* narrative. She used role-play exercises with me to practice stepping back from it. Eventually, she learned how to spot and disengage from her story.

By the time we had completed our sessions, Betty had made the difficult but empowering decision to divorce her husband, who showed no interest in coming to terms with his alcoholism and had also become physically abusive to her. She took a part-time job as a transcriber, enrolled in a night-class law school program, and is now working toward her law degree.

Perhaps most remarkable of all, Betty's physical illness—irritable bowel syndrome—resolved itself. The disorder went away when Betty learned how to deal with the stress in her life more effectively.

Time and time again, I have seen people who had extremely serious physical problems make the same kinds of sudden recoveries. A few decades ago, traditional medical science would have negated the idea of psychological problems manifesting in physical disorders. These days, the medical profession has accepted that effective stress management improves health outcomes. That certainly happened in Betty's case.

> "We let go in order to uncover happiness and peace. We believe that's difficult to let go, but in truth, it is more difficult and painful to hold and protect"— Jiddu Krishnamurti

In the next chapter, you will get a close-up examination of the three steps that made these success stories possible. You will also learn how to implement these three steps in your own life. Before you move on to

Chapter Nine, I want you to try to identify your own story and commit it to writing. *What you come up with should be no more than one sentence long. For instance:* I will sacrifice myself for you, and you will love me. *Use the stories I shared with you in this chapter as points of comparison.*

CHAPTER 9

*Three Components for
Healthy Living*

"What is the meaning of life? To be happy and useful." —The Dalai Lama

ALL THREE OF THE POWERFUL SUCCESS STORIES YOU READ IN Chapter Eight—in fact, all of the success stories I have shared with you in this book—share a simple unifying factor. *Each of the people at the center of the story practiced, mastered, and eventually used the mindfulness response multiple times each day, whenever he or she encountered a minor stressor.* This response became second nature to all of the people you have met in these pages. The mindfulness response made it possible for them to live happier and healthier lives.

Take a look at the mindfulness response once again.

The Mindfulness Response

1. Do not judge. Experience the situation. Intentionally look at what is happening in a nonjudgmental manner.

2. Awareness. Become aware of what you are personally experiencing mentally and physically.

3. Acceptance of the here and now. Accept the situation, and choose what it means to you, right now, so you can respond authentically in the present moment—without judging what is happening.

I know you have seen this process before in this book ... but now my challenge to you is not just to notice it, not just to remember it, but to *internalize* and *apply* it.

Each of the steps of the mindfulness response is a component to healthy living. In fact, if you take a moment to conduct a personal assessment of the people in your own life who are most balanced, I think you will find that some of these individuals already make a habit of the mindfulness response. They may not claim that term of course, but what you call this does not really matter. What matters is whether it is applied it on a regular basis.

Once you have mastered each of the three mindfulness steps and have made it second nature for *you* as you go through your own day, you will find that you, too, are living a happier, healthier, and more fulfilled life.

> "It stands to reason that anyone who learns to live well will die well. The skills are the same: being present in the moment, and humble, and brave, and keeping a sense of humor." —Victoria Moran, *Younger by the Day: 365 Ways to Rejuvenate Your Body and Revitalize Your Spirit*

One good way to internalize and to practice the mindfulness response is to consider each of the steps closely as a question. These questions can change what you consider to be significant in your own life, and they can also change the significance you bring into the lives of others.

Question One: What Is Really Happening Here?

"Be here now."—Ram Dass

You can use this question to *experience the situation and intentionally look at what is happening in a nonjudgmental manner.*

In Lisa's case, she learned to experience Bob's silence in a different way. She had the intention of looking at what was happening in her relationship with Bob without prejudging it, and that intention made all the difference. In time she learned to adjust to Bob's daily rhythms (just as he learned to adjust to hers) and ask, "What's really happening here?" In other words, what did she really know for sure about her situation?

Usually, what Lisa knew for sure about those times when Bob did not feel like talking was that Bob felt like being silent for a bit. That was all.

Question Two: What Am I Experiencing Mentally and Physically?

"Feelings and sensations come and go like clouds in a windy sky."—Thích Nhất Hạnh

You can use this question to *breathe in and become more aware of what you are personally experiencing in your mind and body as you encounter the minor stressor.*

In Lisa's case, this second step was an opportunity to notice where the minor stressor of Bob not wanting to talk was presenting itself physically. Often she felt a certain uncomfortable buzzing in her chest and some tenseness in her shoulder. The simple act of breathing deep, however, and noticing the physical manifestation of the minor stressor was often enough to ease the feeling of being overwhelmed that she had previously associated with Bob not wanting to talk.

Question Three: What Does This Mean to Me Right Now?

> "Remember, the past is history, the future is a mystery. Being alive in this moment is a gift—that is why they call it the present." —Unknown

You can use this question to *accept the situation and choose what it means to you, so you can respond authentically,* right now, *without judging what is happening.*

In Lisa's case, this third step of the mindfulness process allowed her to stop fighting Bob's occasional need for quiet time and evaluate its actual significance more clearly and accurately. With clarity, she was able to assess whether or not Bob's silence really meant that she was facing a crisis in their relationship or that Bob needed his quiet time. After a few weeks of implementing the mindfulness process, she was able to assign the following meaning to Bob's need for quiet time: "Bob becomes closer to me when I respect his need to use silence as his way to de-stress after a long day at work."

This interpretation supported her, supported Bob, and supported the relationship.

Lisa used the mindfulness response to leave her narrative, her story, behind. You can too ... starting right now!

Ask Your Own Questions!

The truly wonderful thing about life is that we get to choose our own questions. The three questions I have just shared with you are gateways to healthy living and happiness. They are worth practicing, internalizing, becoming part of each and every day. They are worth making a part of your relationships with the most important people in your life.

> "One day your entire life will be like a movie in flashback. You just need to make sure that it's worth watching."—Vijay Gandhi

Before you move on to the next chapter, I would like you use the three mindfulness questions I shared with you here to handle at least three different minor stressors in your world. You should be able to find at least three over the next twenty-four hours without any difficulty. Here they are again:

- Question one: What is really happening here?
- Question two: What am I experiencing mentally and physically?
- Question three: What does this mean to me right now?

Do not let the familiarity of these questions become a hurdle for you. The question is not whether you recognize these questions but whether you are using them easily and intuitively. Taking the action I have suggested will help you to internalize what you have learned in this book.

> "Start by doing what is necessary, then do what is possible, and suddenly you are doing the impossible."—St. Francis of Assisi

Let's Keep Going!

In the next chapter, we will look at one of life's biggest questions: *What is happiness?* If you were to ask a hundred people what would make them happy, you would get a lot of different answers. Some people would say money. Others would answer family ties. Others might say belongings. Still others would tell you that happiness is a matter of finding or maintaining the right personal relationships. All of these answers are potentially important, but all of them are incomplete. To sustain happiness in your finances, in your family life, in your social world, in your personal relationships, or in any other part of your life, you need the missing piece that completes the puzzle. To learn what that missing piece is ... keep reading.

CHAPTER 10

What Is Happiness?

*S*OMETIMES WE GET USED TO THINKING OF HAPPINESS AS AN emotion that correlates with material belongings or perhaps with people. Based on my clinical experience, that is not really how it works.

We may imagine that if we get that new car we want or create the kind of relationship we want, with the kind of person we want in our lives, we are going to be happy. Long-term happiness does not correlate strongly with any of those things. Stressful situations still arise even though we have that nice car and are in a good relationship with the right person. The car can get stolen. The relationship can have its ups and downs. The person will change over time. Even though we attain the external thing that we had linked with happiness, we may find that we are not all that happy.

Researchers have shown that people have difficulty predicting how they would feel in response to future events which would lead to happiness or unhappiness. In other words, people tend to overestimate how happy or unhappy they would be as the result of a positive or negative experience.

Timothy Wilson and Daniel Gilbert conducted a study which was published in the journal of *Advances in Experimental Social Psychology*. In their study they wanted to determine how individuals would predict their future emotional responses. They asked various participants to predict how they would feel after various positive and negative life experiences. They then compared their predictions to how others experiencing those events actually felt.

The researchers found that people overestimated the strength and duration of their emotional reactions, which is classically known as *affective forecasting*. An example of this is as follows: how happy would you be if you won the million-dollar lottery? You would probably say very happy. Wilson and Gilbert found that, in actuality, whether you won the lottery or not, one month after that event the level of happiness that each person felt would probably be the same. To challenge this assumption made by Wilson and Gilbert, I recently had a friend who won the mega million-dollar lottery. Literally one month after she won, I asked her if she was happier now than before she had won the lottery. Her response was, "no." Think back to a material item you recently purchased. How happy were you when you first purchased that item? A month after, did you feel the same level of happiness?

It is how we deal with the inevitable stressful moments we experience in life that determines whether we are going to be genuinely happy. Inner happiness involves the ability to harmonize our inner world with the ineluctable and mercurial changes of life.

Happiness correlates directly to mindfulness. Happiness correlates directly to our ability to respond rather than react to what happens in life.

I realize that may seem simplistic, like a generalization that cannot possibly hold up under close examination. It is not. You can test this principle for yourself very easily. When you feel a strong knee-jerk reaction to something—someone who cut you off in traffic, let's say, or a harsh word from a coworker—how do you feel? You will probably feel angry, hurtful, or even sad.

Being in a state of reaction makes it impossible for you to feel fulfilled and resourceful, and it also makes it impossible for you to have exchanges with other people that make them feel fulfilled and resourceful. More importantly, it also makes you lack compassion and empathy. That is what real happiness is: the ability to maintain a sense of well-being and feel fulfilled and resourceful in the present moment, regardless of what that moment brings you. As moments of pleasure and delight will touch our lives and hearts, we will also be asked to respond to loss, failure, and pain. Can we still find internal happiness despite fluctuating life events?

Please do not assume from the title of this book that I am saying that no matter what life throws at you, you must smile as though you were a robot wearing a preprogrammed grin. That is not happiness. That is being a machine.

The point is we have to learn how to create an inner sense of well-being through a mindful response that allows us to stay focused during times of pleasure as well as despair.

Happiness is not mindless cheerfulness. It is a tangible, resourceful result we produce for ourselves when we are able to step back, disengage, reassess, and determine the meaning of what we experience for ourselves.

Moving Beyond the Drama

As you know by now, reacting to something is a very different experience from consciously responding to it. Whenever you respond to something consciously using the mindfulness response, you will find that you can engage without the full range of emotions, without the past stories, and without the drama.

When you *react*, my guess is like most of us, you will tend to react by producing drama. Who is right? Who is wrong? Who did what, and who let whom down? Your stories of people and events can create lots and lots of drama. (I know, because mine can, too.) That is not going to change. But your ability to notice the stories when they pop up *can* change.

After decades of work with thousands of people, I have come to believe that for those of us who want to experience true happiness, it is far better to learn to respond authentically to the situations we encounter in our lives than to heedlessly *react* to those situations.

Once you have the answers to these questions, I predict you will be ready to experience the mindfulness response for yourself and create happiness (internal well-being) in your own life.

"What Do You Do?"

It is quite common for people to ask me what I do for a living. I used to say, "I help people deal with stress." Lately, I have been responding differently to that question: "I help people learn how to respond rather than react to situations. And in doing that, I give them the key to something all of us really want: happiness."

> If your aim in life is to experience happiness on a consistent basis, I suggest you take personal responsibility for answering these questions: What puts me into reaction? What stories appear when I go into reaction? Who really controls my thoughts and actions?

Dealing with Negative Thoughts During the Day

Just knowing that you want to respond rather than react is not a magic bullet. The reality is that each of us is going to have reactive stress-driven thoughts as we make our way through the average day. With the mindfulness response, we can learn to let them be *fleeting* thoughts, learn to let them come and let them go. It is when we hold on to negative knee-jerk reactions that we create drama, which develops into a series of sequels.

Please understand; I am not saying this is something you are going master by tomorrow morning. It takes practice, but it begins with awareness. Awareness means simply being able to step back and say, "I have seen this before; I know what is happening to me." This is a lifelong process. It also takes an open mind or what I like to refer to as a beginner's mind. A beginner's mind allows you to encounter each situation with openness and a willingness to respond rather than react.

The process of introspection allows us to examine ourselves and our thoughts and actions. We may find that we are more resourceful than we realize in turning around old patterns of thought and action. Just because something has a long history does not mean it has to be a life sentence.

We may be able to find a place of patience and compassion with ourselves as we get better at adopting the mindfulness response. We may get better at giving ourselves some time to practice this. After all, we are reconditioning and reprogramming behaviors that we have been practicing for a very long time. Change is not going to happen overnight. It takes practice. It takes dedication. It takes patience.

> Happiness is not a quick fix. Quick fixes are called *pleasures,* which come and go. Happiness that is dependent upon pleasure is external happiness. We are striving for inner happiness.

In my experience people can be their own personal inner life consultant. And everyone can create her own personal program for dealing with situations. All people need their own operating manual. My challenge to you as this book draws to a close is a simple one. I want you to assume personal responsibility for creating that operating manual. To do that, you will have to learn what works and what does not work when it comes to maintaining your own balance and supporting your own best responses to stress.

Where Happiness Begins

Happiness begins when you start to feel grateful and appreciative for all the moments and experiences you encounter in life. The Buddha said it quite simply: "The source of happiness and unhappiness lies nowhere else but in our minds and hearts." He further stated that we discover happiness through making peace with ourselves and the circumstances of our lives, not trying to escape from them nor through living in fantasies about the future. We can make peace with our lives through learning to connect with the simple truths of each moment.

Everybody—and I do mean everybody—can have an aha moment no matter how long they have been engaging in a pattern of behavior that does not support them. Here's the catch, though. No one else can gain insight for you. You have to gain insight for yourself.

Here is the good news: You are stronger and more resourceful than you think. When you learn to use the mindfulness response to help yourself, you will develop more empathy and compassion, which will help you in your interpersonal relationships. You will gain more clarity, and you will get better at helping others create mindful responses to the events in *their* lives.

Do not let the destination become more important than the journey. Stay mindful, and stay in the moment!

Appendix A:
Thought Process Worksheet

Use this worksheet to identify unhealthy thoughts that you commonly experience each day. This worksheet will assist you in transitioning from unhealthy thinking to positive thinking. For each unhealthy thought identified, replace it with a healthy or neutral thought. This exercise is best done at the end of the day.

Identify unhealthy thoughts (Example: "I am unlovable.")

1. _____
2. _____
3. _____
4. _____
5. _____

Healthy replacement thoughts (Example: "I am loving and loved.")

1. _____
2. _____
3. _____
4. _____
5. _____

Behavioral changes (if applicable) (Example: Expressed unconditional caring affection for someone who is close to you.)

1. _____
2. _____
3. _____
4. _____
5. _____

Appendix B:
Incident Worksheet

*S*ometimes incidents trigger reactions that do not necessarily support healthy, conscious responses to our situation. Use the worksheet below to engage in self-introspection on a recent incident.

Incident: State only the facts about what occurred. Do not share feelings or emotions about the incident. (For example, "He wants a divorce.")

_____
_____
_____
_____
_____
_____
_____
_____

Feelings about incident: State how you feel about incident. (For example, "I feel sad, angry, upset.")

_____
_____
_____
_____
_____
_____
_____
_____

Behavior: How did you respond to the incident? (For example, "I yelled at her." Or, "I started drinking.")

_____

_____

_____

_____

_____

_____

_____

_____

Knowing what you know now, what would you have done differently regarding this incident? (For example, "I would have left the house instead of arguing.")

_____

_____

_____

_____

_____

_____

_____

_____

Appendix C:
Ten Simple Ways to Be Happy

*H*ere are ten simple things you can do right now to bring about happiness in your life. How many can you turn into a daily personal experience?

1. **Practice mindfulness.** Be in the moment. Instead of worrying about your medical checkup tomorrow while you have dinner with your family, focus on the here and now—the food, the company, and the conversation.

2. **Laugh out loud.** Just anticipating a happy, funny event can raise the levels of endorphins and other pleasure-inducing hormones ... and lower the production of stress-related hormones.

3. **Do one thing at a time.** People who try to multitask are more likely to have high blood pressure. Take that to heart! Instead of talking on the phone while you fold laundry or clean the kitchen, sit down in a comfortable chair and turn your entire attention over to the conversation. Instead of checking e-mail as you work on other projects, turn off the e-mail function until you finish what you're doing. (This is similar to the concept of mindfulness.)

4. **Take the dog for a walk.** Interact with any beloved pet. There are numerous studies that attest to the stress-relieving benefits of pets. In one analysis, researchers evaluated the heart health of 240 couples, half of whom owned a pet. Couples with pets had significantly lower heart rates and blood pressure levels when exposed to stressors than the couples who did not have pets. In fact, the pets were even more effective at buffering stress than the spouses were.

5. **Count your blessings.** People who pause each day to reflect on some positive aspect of their lives (health, friends, family, freedom, education, etc.) tend to experience a heightened sense of well-being.

6. **Try volunteering.** Research suggests that when we are altruistic, we tend to feel happier. Helping others can counteract feelings of sadness.

7. **Stop comparing yourself to others.** Evaluating your abilities and opinions by comparing yourself to others makes you less resourceful when it comes to dealing with stress.

8. **Develop a social support network.** Loneliness has been correlated with unhappiness. People who have a good social support network tend to report feeling happier and more able to cope effectively with life's challenges.

9. **Learn to let go.** Sometimes you have to let go in order to find peace and happiness in your life. Letting go may mean dissolving an unhealthy relationship, letting go of the need to always be in control, or simply letting go of an unfilled desire or want.

10. **Challenge yourself to do something differently.** Vary the daily routine. One simple change in your life, such as taking a different route home from work, can create a positive and healthy sense of well-being, simply by promoting a deeper awareness of what you are doing.

Appendix D:
From Wherever You
Are to Happiness

*L*et's face it. Life's everyday hassles can be a distraction. When I have found myself distracted, these affirmations have helped me to get back on track with the mindfulness response. I have been collecting these sayings for over two decades. I believe they can help to lead you from wherever you are to happiness. For your convenience I organized these affirmations in the following categories: Anger, Compassion, Happiness, and Motivation.

Anger

"You will not be punished for your anger, you will be punished by your anger." —Buddha

"For every minute you remain angry, you give up sixty seconds of peace of mind." —Ralph Waldo Emerson

"When anger rises, think of the consequences." —Confucius

"Get mad, then get over it." —Colin Powell

Compassion

"I've learned that people will forget what you said, people will forget what you did, but people will never forget how you made them feel." —Maya Angelou

"You cannot teach a man anything. You can only help him to find it within himself." —Galileo

"As we become less of an expert on the other, we become more of an expert on the self." —Harriet Lerner

"Everyone thinks of changing the world, but no one thinks of changing himself." —Leo Tolstoy

"One should learn to judge without being judgmental." —Unknown

Happiness

"Suffering usually relates to wanting things to be different from the way they are." —Allan Lokos, *Pocket Peace: Effective Practices for Enlightened Living*

"Most folks are as happy as they make their minds up to be." —Abraham Lincoln

"If you want to be happy; be." —Leo Tolstoy

"Happiness is when what you think, what you say, and what you do are in harmony." —Mahatma Gandhi

"Be happy in the moment, that's enough. Each moment is all we need, not more." —Mother Teresa

"Sacrifice with no likelihood of accompanying happiness is pathological and absurd." —Unknown

"If you really want to remove a cloud from your life, you do not make a big production of it, you just relax and remove it from your thinking. That's all there is to it." —Richard Bach, *Illusions: The Adventures of a Reluctant Messiah*

"Happiness is not something ready-made. It comes from your own actions." —Dalai Lama

"I find hope in the darkest of days, and focus in the brightest. I do not judge the universe." —Dalai Lama

"The most important thing is to enjoy life—to be happy—it's all that matters." —Audrey Hepburn

Motivation

"Stay present for the 'now' of your life. It's your 'point of power.'" —Doug Dillon

"Live for today but prepare for tomorrow." —Anonymous

"Perseverance .... Never give up, for that is the place and the time that the tide will turn." —Unknown

"We become what we contemplate." —Plato

"Life is a boomerang. What you give, you get back." —Dale Carnegie

"If you don't like something, change it. If you can't change it, change your attitude." —Maya Angelou

"Don't seek, don't search, don't ask, don't knock, don't demand—relax. If you relax it comes." —Osho

"You should sit in meditation for twenty minutes every day
- unless you're too busy;
- then you should sit for an hour."
—Old Zen adage

"Everything has its wonders, even darkness and silence, and I learn, whatever state I may be in, therein to be content." —Helen Keller

"Once you replace negative thoughts with positive ones, you'll start having positive results." —Willie Nelson

"Always turn a negative situation into a positive situation." —Michael Jordan

"I have just three things to teach: simplicity, patience, and compassion. These three are the greatest treasures." —Lao Tzu

"Don't dwell on what went wrong. Instead, focus on what to do next. Spend your energies on moving forward toward finding the answer." —Denis Waitley

"With the new day comes new strength and new thoughts." —Eleanor Roosevelt

"Optimism is the faith that leads to achievement. Nothing can be done without hope and confidence."
—Helen Keller

"After a storm comes a calm." —Matthew Henry

"The more you praise and celebrate your life, the more there is in life to celebrate." —Oprah Winfrey

NOTES

NOTES

.

References

Antoninus, Marcus Aurelius. *Meditations: Marcus Aurelius*. England: Penguin, 1964.

Bach, Richard. Illusions: *The Adventures of a Reluctant Messiah*. New York: Delacorte, 1977.

Chan, Amanda L. "Mindfulness Meditation Benefits: 20 Reasons Why It's Good For Your Mental and Physical Health." *The Huffington Post*. February 18, 2013. http://huffingtonpost.com

Chopra, Deepak. *The Book of Secrets: Unlocking the Hidden Dimensions of Your Life*. New York: Harmony, 2004.

Cole, Ralley. *This Is Water*. New York: Mondo, 2004.

Dass, Ram. *Be Here Now*. New York: Crown, 1971.

De Mello, Anthony *Awakening: Conversations with the Masters*. Image, 2003.

Dines, Christopher. *Mindfulness Meditation:* London. La Petite Fleur Publishing, 2014.

Griffith, R. M. "*10 Health Problems Related to Stress That You Can Fix.*' Sri Lanka Newspapers, December 4, 2010.

Hạnh, Thích Nhất. *Stepping into Freedom: An Introduction to Buddhist Monastic Training*. Berkeley: Parallax, 1997.

Huston, Matt. "*Help Yourself! Positive thinking has become a staple of.*

But how well does it actually work?" Psychology Today, January 01, 2014.

Kornfield, Jack. *A Path with Heart: A Guide through the Perils and Promises of Spiritual Life.* New York: Bantam, 1993.

Kotler, Arnold. *Peace Is Every Step: The Path of Mindfulness in Everyday Life.* New York: Bantam, 1991.

Levine, Stephen. *A Year to Live: How to Live This Year as If It Were Your Last.* New York: Bell Tower, 1997.

Lokos, Allan. *Patience: The Art of Peaceful Living.* New York: Tarcher/ Penguin, 2012.

"Meditation, Exercise Could Protect You From The Flu." *The Huffington Post.* July 14, 2012. http://huffingtonpost.com

Mikulka, Charlette. *Peace in the Heart & Home: A Down-to-Earth Guide to Creating a Better Life for You and Your Loved Ones.* Newton, NJ: Kittacanoe, 2011.

Mobi Ho, and Dinh Mai. Vo. *The Miracle of Mindfulness: An Introduction to the Practice of Meditation.* Boston: Beacon, 1987.

Moran, Victoria. *Younger by the Day: 365 Ways to Rejuvenate Your Body and Revitalize Your Spirit.* San Francisco: Harper San Francisco, 2004.

National Center for Biotechnology Information. U.S. National Library of Medicine, *Result Filters.,* accessed April 13, 2014 http://ncbi.nim.nih.gov.

O'Reilley, Mary Rose. *The Barn at the End of the World: The*

Apprenticeship of a Quaker, Buddhist Shepherd. Minneapolis: Milkweed Editions, 2000.

Patañjali. *Yoga Sutras.* Calcutta: S. Gupta, 1963.

Pocket Peace: Effective Practices for Enlightened Living. New York: Tarcher/Penguin, 2010.

Ray, Amit. *Om Chanting and Meditation: A Way to Health and Happiness.* Lexington, KY: Inner Light, 2010.

Richo, David. *When the Past Is Present: Healing the Emotional Wounds That Sabotage Our Relationships.* Boston: Shambhala, 2008.

Watts, Alan. *Psychotherapy, East and West.* New York: Pantheon, 1961.

Wilson, T. D. and Gilbert, D. T. *"Affective Forecasting." Journal Advances in Experimental Social Psychology* 35, 345-411.

About the Author

*D*EBORAH C. MOORE, PhD, IS A LICENSED MARRIAGE AND family therapist and life coach. She empowers and motivates individuals and couples to achieve important goals. Since retiring from the New York City Police Department, she has been active in developing programs to promote health and well-being. A self-proclaimed "neuropsychotherapist," Dr. Moore has spent over 20 years researching how mismanaged stress shaves years off of your life. Her practice integrates cognitive behavioral techniques, neuroscience, and mindful-based training to assist individuals.

Dr. Moore travels to different locations promoting her techniques for developing inner happiness and mindfulness. Her presentations are interactive, stimulating, and solution-focused, often leaving participants with that "aha" feeling.

For more information about Dr. Moore's services or to book an event, please visit www.drdebimoore.com.

CPSIA information can be obtained at www.ICGtesting.com
Printed in the USA
BVOW05s0604191114

375691BV00001B/60/P